HOW CHRISTIAN

Are You?

RICHARD J. HART, OFM Cap

Paulist Press
New York/Mahwah, NJ

Cover and book design by Lynn Else

Library of Congress Cataloging-in-Publication Data

Hart, Richard, OFM Cap.
  How Christian are you? / Richard Hart.
     p. cm.
  Includes bibliographical references (p.   ).
  ISBN 978-0-8091-4579-9 (alk. paper)
  1. Christian life—Catholic authors. I. Title.
  BX2350.3.H37 2009
  248.4´82—dc22

                                                    2008045485

Published by Paulist Press
997 Macarthur Boulevard
Mahwah, New Jersey 07430

www.paulistpress.com

Printed and bound in the
United States of America

CONTENTS

iv ♨ CONTENTS

ACKNOWLEDGMENTS

This small book is the result of people who encouraged me to write it, especially those who heard me preach at parish renewals. It is not intended to be a scholarly work.

I want to thank sincerely Ellen O'Brien, who offered some very helpful suggestions and corrections.

Also, a word of thanks to Rev. Michael Kerrigan, CSP, of Paulist Press for his encouragement as well as his insightful suggestions on how to improve this book.

Special thanks to the many people who supported me by their prayers, inspiring lives, and friendship while writing this labor of love.

Finally, I would like to dedicate this book to my mother, Sylvia Bucher.

Richard J. Hart, OFM Cap

INTRODUCTION

When I told a woman friend the title of this book, she declared, "I do not want to read it!" That might have been your initial reaction as well.

Isn't it true that many of us claim we are Christians but we often are not any different from others in our religious beliefs and lifestyle? Have we closed the gap between what we profess and what Jesus calls us to be?

Reading this book may feel like stepping on some toes and causing us to wince. How willing are we to face the truth that many of us are *not* living the Gospel? Examining how Christian we are might act as strong medicine to swallow, but the prescription will help us to be more *Christlike*.

As Christians, we need to be more influential upon society. Has the salt of our lives lost its flavor? Have we become spiritually impotent, have we been paralyzed by cheap grace, or have we grown lukewarm? Do we act in a countercultural way to our society against individualism, materialism, sexism, and racism?

We claim Jesus is Lord with our mouths, but do our actions often demonstrate how we are more attracted to self-fulfillment, money, power, and sex? Are we becoming more like the world we seek to change? Do our words match our deeds? Or, do we use cover-ups: lying becomes face saving, greed becomes retirement planning, murder becomes compassion for the terminally ill, pride becomes self-esteem?

How seriously do we take the Christian life? How Christian are we? The early Christians were exposed to ridicule, persecution, and death. What enabled them to accept this abuse was the realization of how deeply God loved them. Once we feel deeply, not just think, how much God loves us, there is a readiness to accept suffering and persecution. The more we feel God's love, the more we will show love toward others, our neighbor. The early Christians were known by their way of acting: "Look how they love one another."

Our task is to transform the straight lines of our life into a triangle of love with the Trinity as its foundation, enabling us to love the way Jesus loved. The Bishops in Australia have launched a pastoral letter, *Go Tell Everyone,* that points out how this Christian challenge has never been greater or more important than now. Who is our neighbor? How do we respond to "Go, and do likewise"? A true Christian does not ration out one's love to others.

Truly, Christianity is presently at the crossroads and maybe the signposts are no longer there to show us the way. That is an added reason why we need to discipline ourselves to follow the less traveled road that Jesus has mapped out for us. It is much easier to take the super highway rather than the narrow road. If discipline is closely allied to discipleship, we need to take seriously Christ's invitation to live as his disciple as fully as possible. How willing are we to follow Jesus wherever he might lead us or whatever he might ask of us? That challenge might entail finding a balance between tolerance and intolerance, or accepting the dark side of enmity and overcoming it.

Historian Martin Kugler has launched a program entitled *Europe for Christ,* whose objective is to embolden Christians to influence the development of Europe. He maintains that a future without Christ is unthinkable. He also claims that too many

Christians are living in their own ghetto created by their own indifference and lack of hope. Is that true of us?

We might be *care-fronted* in these areas and then have to ask ourselves how willing am I to *care-front* others when necessary. The gospel counsel of *care-frontation* is one that few Christians accomplish well because of the fears involved. We might need to be nudged in this important area, and especially the radical area of forgiveness. We can claim to be a giving Christian, but how forgiving are we? Christianity is a way of walking, not just talking. We need to do some soul searching about how forgiving we are of others and especially ourselves. That is an imposing challenge.

Much will depend on our attitude toward life and ourselves. Attitude is everything. Some Christians look upon Christ's teachings as a tasteless syrup or a pabulum, so they pick and choose and become "cafeteria Christians." We are called to adopt Christ's attitude by accepting all his teachings that challenge us to risk our own lives. Christians need to be countercultural.

Jesus preached and taught much about money and wealth, but conflicting opinions concerning wealth do exist. We must never accept a watered-down version of the gospel concerning greed or what Jesus said, "Do not store up for yourselves treasures on earth..." (Matt 6:19). We might interpret this by saying that it really doesn't matter how much money I make as long as I don't get snobbish or stuck up. Christians need to set a higher bar than that and be more sharing and caring of others.

Rich people are often considered insiders, whereas poor people are outsiders. How do we react or treat aliens, strangers, and immigrants? As Christians, there is a need to be on the cutting edge when addressing this thorny problem. A comparable problem is how to treat children properly. Children are the future of the world and need the respect, care, and love of all people, especially parents, so we cannot stand on the sidelines when we see the injustices done to them.

Once prayer becomes a priority in our lives it will enable us to overcome the difficulties we might face—not enough time, distractions, restlessness, spiritual aridity, and poor listening skills. It is an endless adventure. By praying we explore the inner caverns of our lives, realizing more fully how much God loves us and wants us to show God's love to others. Our love for God, others, and ourselves will determine how Christian we really are.

1

GOD OUR LOVER

"Because you are precious in my sight and honored, and I love you."
Isa 43:4

Pope Benedict XVI surprised many Christians as well as others with his first encyclical *Deus Caritas Est* ("God Is Love"). It did not contain, as some had hoped, statements on controversial issues like sexual morality, ordination of women, homosexual unions, and liturgical. No condemnatory statements are found in it concerning a "culture of death."[1] His statements are made in a positive and respectful context rather than with harsh judgments.

Some Christians perceive God as an avenger, a punisher, or an unyielding judge rather than a lover who looks on the world with compassion and divine love. Philosopher Father Jesus Villagasa believes that the pope's encyclical might spark a revolution of love and definitely is a treasure of wisdom. He marvels how the pope shows the similarities and differences between divine and human love. He believes that only God's love can transform the world.

If we could summarize the whole Bible in a few words, it would be "God is love." George Elliott, a famous writer, insisted that telling him he was loved is not as important *as being loved*. The Bible is God's love story that keeps telling us that God loves us. God's love is unique. We will not find this *agape* or self-giving love anywhere else. God's love is unconditional, with no strings attached.

Did you ever notice that Jesus never said to Bartimaeus once his eyesight was restored, "Now, don't go around eyeing beautiful women?" Or to the man whose hand was restored, "Now, don't go out and steal?" Human love is conditional and limited while God's love is as limitless as space, with no boundaries, and as bottomless as the ocean. God's love is also everlasting, as Jeremiah proclaimed, "I have loved you with an everlasting love" (Jer 31:3). God speaks through Isaiah, "with everlasting love I will have compassion on you," and "My steadfast love shall not depart from you" (Isa 54:8, 10). Hosea spoke of God's love for Israel as "I will take you for my wife forever; I will take you for my wife in righteousness and in justice, in steadfast love, and in mercy" (Hos 2:19). The constant refrain of Psalm 136 is "His steadfast love endures forever." Everything seems temporary and can easily disappear, but God's love is permanent. God's love is also relentless as exemplified so well in Francis Thompson's *The Hound of Heaven*. We might flee from God, even for years, but God's love never stops pursuing us until we are loved into submission.

No love here on earth can compare to God's love, even a mother's love for a child. Isaiah expressed it well, "Can a mother forget her nursing child, or show no compassion for the child of her womb? Even these may forget, yet I will not forget you" (Isa 49:15). We hear or read of stories where mothers abandon their children, or, even more tragically, kill them. God will never abandon any of us, "Because you are precious in my sight, and honored, and I love you" (Isa 43:4). The psalmist says, "But you, O Lord, are a God merciful and gracious, slow to anger and abounding in steadfast love and faithfulness" (Ps 86:15). And again, "How precious is your steadfast love, O God" (Ps 36:7). God will not let go of us because our existence depends on God's love.

Exclusive and Personal Love

God's love is an exclusive love for us, as if we were the only person on earth. Only God can do that. God has loved us even before we have existed; as Jeremiah said, "Before I formed you in the womb I knew you" (Jer 1:5). As the psalmist exclaimed, "For it was you who formed my inward parts; you knit me together in my mother's womb" (Ps 139:13). In Deuteronomy, we read that God chose the Jews not because they "were more numerous than any other people that the Lord set his heart on you and chose you" (Deut 7:7). Hilaire Belloc expressed it well when he said that it was odd of God to choose the Jews.

Song of Songs portrays God in human love as a lover of his people. The author paints a beautiful picture of Israel as the chosen people whom God loves. Pope Benedict XVI states in his encyclical *Deus Caritas Est* that these love songs in final analysis describe God's love for us and our love for God. Marriage is used as a symbol by the author of *Song of Songs* as well as the mystics who wrote about God's love. John of the Cross and Teresa of Avila wrote of it as "bridal mysticism," stressing the relationship of lover and beloved. Pope Benedict XVI in his encyclical calls the *Song of Songs* "a source of mystical knowledge and experience" (no. 10).

God's love is shown to us through Adam and Eve, who did not ask for forgiveness once they had sinned. Even so, God takes the initiative and promises a redeemer, a savior of the world. Again, God shows his love to Cain, who out of jealousy kills his brother Abel. Cain feels that his punishment of being a restless wanderer is too great to bear. God assures him of protection, however, by saying, "Whoever kills Cain will suffer a sevenfold vengeance" (Gen 4:15).

God showed love to Noah and his family by sparing them from the flood and assuring Noah that the earth would not be destroyed again by a flood. God loved Abram and called him out of Haran to Canaan. God then promised him that Sarah, who was beyond childbearing age, would conceive, and that his descendants would be as numerous as the stars in the heavens and the sands on the seashore.

God preserved Moses' life and gave him a glimpse of God's love in the burning bush. God showed love for the Israelites in their affliction in Egypt by sending Moses to the Pharaoh. When Moses finally convinced the Pharaoh to let his people go, Moses, with God's help, led them through the Red Sea. This became the one event that the people never forgot. God continued to show love by guiding the Israelites through the desert "in a pillar of cloud by day, to lead them along the way, and a pillar of fire by night, to give them light" (Exod 13:21). God gave the manna and then the quail as he accompanied them to the promised land.

God's love has not been written on tablets of stone for us, but on each one of our fleshly hearts. God loves us more than we love ourselves. We need to be more surprised by how much God loves us. Thomas Merton wrote to a religious sister who was a friend of his that she had to realize more fully how much God loved her, and how basic that was to her belief. He felt that all the great mysteries of redemption will have an influence on us only as far as we see them manifesting God's love. St. John in his epistle writes, "In this is love, not that we loved God but that he loved us and sent his Son to be the atoning sacrifice for our sins. So we have known and believe the love God has for us. God is love, and those who abide in love abide in God, and God abides in them" (1 John 4:10, 16).

One of the best-known Latin American hymns is "Lord, you have looked into my eyes; smiling, you have called my name." It poignantly describes how God has first loved us, and recalls

Isaiah's words, "I call you by your name" (Isa 45:4). This is Christianity's core belief that God has first loved us. Christ looks upon us, smiling, and calls us by our name. We who are so unworthy have become worthy because of God's love. This is not a cruel hoax, but all the articles of our Christian faith become a footnote to this basic belief. Believing in God's love for us becomes the essence of our faith. Faith must allay any of our fears of allowing God to love us and give us the courage to be more open to God's love that is not abstract but very personal and intimate. Is this happening?

Some Christians find it hard to believe this personal and exclusive love, especially when they consider all the people in the world, or when they consider their own sinfulness and inadequacies. How could God possibly love them?

Often, I have heard individuals tell me that they find it hard to accept human love saying, "If only the person knew me." That is the beauty of God's love, that God knows us better than we know ourselves or anyone else and still loves us. The deeper our faith grows the more we will understand this truth. William Coffin believes that Christians with reckless faith take the leap and then grow wings. If we were at the edge of an abyss, would we step backward or forward?

Many of us think God will love us if and when we change. God, however, loves us so we can change. Maybe it becomes easier to beat our breasts than to stick out our neck. However, some keep on resisting and find it difficult to accept this stunning reality that God is in love with them. God delights in us as Zephaniah stated, "He will rejoice over you with gladness, he will renew you in his love" (Zeph 3:17). I often ask individuals what is harder, to love or be loved. They finally have to admit that it is harder to be loved because you are not in control.

God's Love Is Different

God's love is different from human love. It is deeper, more intimate, and unconditional. That is an added reason why some find it difficult to grasp or understand it. A quantum leap of faith is needed at times to accept God's love fully. The highest kind of love asks nothing in return, and this is the kind of love God shows us. I remember asking a religious sister on a retreat what she considered her greatest gift. She replied, "Being raised by very loving parents."

Not all children, however, are that fortunate, especially today. Many have experienced a lack of love or had to earn their love by good grades in school or good behavior. Others have been sexually abused by a parent, another family member, or relative. Naturally they will find it more difficult to accept God's love, and they will probably need much professional help to understand how God loves them despite these depersonalizing situations. It takes a tremendous amount of faith to believe that God can be present in these terrible situations. God's love does not depend on what we do in return no matter how noble this might be, or how many talents we possess, or how pretty or handsome we are.

His Holiness Pope Benedict XVI recently said that God loves all individuals regardless of their beauty, intelligence, health, youth, and integrity. He also exclaimed to two hundred thousand pilgrims at the Polish national shrine of Joanna Gora, on May 26, 2006, that what is most important about God is that God is love!

As Peter Van Breemen, SJ, states, "God's love is based on nothing."[2] He means by this that God's love extends to us personally because of our uniqueness. We do not, however, elicit this love because of the good life we are leading or the many acts of kindness shown to others. This love was there before we existed. Gerald May maintains that "love is the core of everything in the theology of Teresa and John. It is the sole purpose of all creation and of us as human beings."[3]

St. John expressed God's love well, "For God so loved the world that he gave us his only Son" (John 3:16). This was the Father's most precious gift to us. Can we think of a better gift than that? Jesus' birth was the greatest love story ever written. John, however, penned it in just a few words, "And the Word became flesh and lived among us" (John 1:14). Those words, like a magic carpet, sweep us back to the garden where we find the first man, Adam, the first woman, Eve, the first sin, and the first blush. Satan tried to poison's God's plan of love for us, but God's love will always be stronger than any evil.

The incarnation means that God is in constant relationship with us. Only in his coming does the Bible have much meaning to us. The Bible has many beautiful stories and the answers to many significant questions, but not all of them are answered as some maintain. William Coffin writes, "The Bible is something like a mirror: if an ass peers in, you can't expect an apostle to look out."[4] Isn't it true that we never tire of hearing the story of Jesus' birth because it is an acted-out parable according to Joachim Jeremias? No wonder Saint Francis of Assisi wanted to act it out because it had such a profound effect on him.

We affirm with Saint John that Jesus is God's revelation, that we can know God in a far more personal and intimate way now. Jesus is Emmanuel, God with us, in all our uncertainties and the injustices found in our troubled world. Once we feel God's love, we will be able to live with certainty rather than uncertainty in our unsettled age. If Jesus incarnates God, Herod incarnates evil by killing innocent children. We still have the Herods with us killing the innocent unborn: children from Thailand being sold as prostitutes to very rich Westerners and death squads in Brazil murdering innocent children are just two examples. Yet Karl

Rahner insists that despite all the division, poverty, brutality, and sinfulness in the world, and sometimes in our hearts, we can still say God is infinite love.

Jesus was willing to give up his glory for our sake and become a human being. St. Paul stated, "Who, though he was in the form of God, did not regard equality with God as something to be exploited, but emptied himself, taking the form of a slave, being born in human likeness" (Phil 2:6–7). He came as a help-less child, concealed his power in swaddling clothes. Our tiny planet became sacred ground like the ground Moses walked on as God said to Moses, "the place on which you are standing is holy ground" (Exod 3:5). As someone has said, imagine earth offering a cave to the Inaccessible. Such love should make us tremble because there is no way to return it. Handel's Messiah begins with "For unto us a child is born," and builds to a thun-derous "and his name shall be called Wonderful."

Jesus Shows The Father's Love

Jesus was indeed "wonderful," showing us the Father's love by his life's mission that he declared in the Nazareth synagogue: "The Spirit of the Lord is upon me, because he has anointed me to bring good news to the poor. He has sent me to proclaim release to the captives and recovery of sight to the blind, to let the oppressed go free, to proclaim the year of the Lord's favor" (Luke 4:18–19).

Indeed, he showed the Father's love by his many miracles of mercy and love, thirty-nine or more that are recorded in the gospels. He cured Peter's mother-in-law, and, as Saint Mark tells us, "That evening, at sundown, they brought to him all who were sick or possessed with demons. And the whole city was gathered around the door. And he cured many who were sick with various diseases, and cast out many demons, and he would not permit the demons to speak, because they knew him" (Mark 1:32–34). Jesus not only cured the paralytic but forgave his sins, which becomes a turning point in the gospels. Up until this time, he cured people but did not forgive sins.

Jesus called ordinary fishermen to come follow him, and they did. Why would they be so willing to do that immediately? Outside of Matthew, the tax collector, they were a motley group of men. Las Vegas would not have bet on them to be the future princes of the church. However, Jesus saw something in them that was special, just as he sees similar qualities in us that are attractive. How often did he have to remind them of his mission of going up to Jerusalem to suffer and die? They could not grasp what this act of love meant. How many of us would have grasped his message had we been there? Do we grasp the full impact of that message now?

Jesus showed his love by reaching out to sinners and outcasts, prostitutes, lepers, and tax collectors like Zacchaeus. Jesus was not afraid to touch lepers even though to do so at that time meant that you were socially unclean. While conducting a parish renewal in Louisiana, I visited the only leprosarium that I know of here in the United States. I actually saw some lepers and found out that they made articles for the neighboring stores. I wondered how many people would buy them if they knew where they came from. Would you?

Saint Francis of Assisi had a great horror of lepers at one time in his life. Every time that he saw a leper, he would scamper away. One day he was touched deeply by God's love and he embraced a leper. That gesture became the turning point in his life. Some of us also might have a leper list, people whom we will not have much to do with or even with whom we speak. God's love has to inspire us also to reach out to them.

My Christmas list of friends is rather lengthy, but I have to ask myself whom I am excluding from that list. Someone who had a difficult time reaching out to lepers and AIDS people is Ferdinand Mahfood who started Food for the Poor, an international non-profit Christian aid organization. On his first visit to Haiti he did not want to touch any of them. So he prayed to overcome his revulsion, which he did by first shaking hands with them and then hugging them. How many of us would be willing to follow his example? Jesus can transform us as he did Saint Francis or Father Damien, the church's best known minister to lepers.

Saint Paul asks: "Who will separate us from the love of Christ? Will hardship, or distress, or persecution, or famine, or nakedness, or peril, or sword? ...No, in all these things we are more than conquerors through him who loved us" (Rom 8:35, 37). He was convinced that nothing could separate us from God's love in Christ Jesus. The only thing that can separate us is ourselves, our pettiness, and our selfishness. We are the only ones who turn away and at times isolate ourselves from God. Jesus' love can conquer that also.

Jesus' Passion and Death Shows His Love

Mark tells us that Jesus "began to teach them that the Son of Man must undergo great suffering, and be rejected by the elders, the chief priests, and the scribes, and be killed, and after three days rise again" (Mark 8:31). This was Jesus' mission, because his love for us urged him to complete the journey to Jerusalem. He was committed to his mission.

Film directors admit that it is easier to portray love as an experience than love as a commitment. Jesus summarized his whole mission to Pilate, "For this I was born, and for this I came into the world, to testify to the truth. Everyone who belongs to the truth listens to my voice" (John 18:37). Jesus embodied the truth of divine love and brought it to the world. He revealed the incomprehensible mystery that God is love.

Henri Nouwen points out how "the truth of which Jesus speaks is not a thesis, or a doctrine, or an intellectual explanation of reality. It is the very relationship, the life-giving intimacy between himself and the Father of which he wants us to partake."[5] How willing are we?

When seeing the crucifix, some Christians respond, "My lover has been crucified." Jesus said, "No one has greater love than this, to lay down one's life for one's friends" (John 15:13). Jesus "walked the talk." What he said he would do, he did. No empty promises. Jesus never asked us to do something that he had not done. He loved us to the very end; as Saint John put it, "Having loved his own who were in the world, he loved them to the end" (John13:1). This really is the key to the passion and death of Jesus. We could meditate on this passage for a lifetime and not exhaust it. Even if you or I had been the only person on earth, Jesus would still have died for us. Jesus' love is the plumb line by which everything should be measured. Jesus challenged us to the highest kind of love, a true love more demanding than laws. He was harsh on the scribes and Pharisees because of their legalism.

Our challenge is to immerse ourselves more deeply into Jesus' passion. The more we share and immerse ourselves into the passion of Jesus, the more we will share his compassion with others. This was certainly true of Julian of Norwich, a mystic of the fourteenth century, who wrote that she believed it was in our Lord's passion where she learned the true meaning of love and love for others. She also believed that God's love for us never slackened and never will.

Saint Paul put it well: "Indeed, rarely will anyone die for a righteous person—though perhaps for a good person someone might actually dare to die. But God proves his love for us in that while we still were sinners Christ died for us" (Rom 5:7–8). We owed a debt we could not pay, but he paid a debt he did not owe. Jesus did not say to us, "If you change your life and clean up your act, I will love you." We don't have to make promises to God before God loves us.

In looking at the cross, we can better understand how precious we are in God's sight. If we possess a low-self image, we can gaze at the cross and remember how worthy we are of his love. But we question how could we be worthy of so much love? God and our parents brought us into existence and helped us to our goal of eternal life that Jesus promised to us. Saint Paul makes it clear to his fellow Christians, "for whom Christ died are destroyed" (1 Cor 8:11). So Jesus died for each one of us, no matter what our status, rich or poor, old or young, attractive or ugly. Jesus died to bring us all together, "to gather into one the dispersed children of God" (John 11:52). Is this really happening in the world, in our lives?

Feeling God's Love

The real task for many Christians is not just to think that God loves them, but to *feel* this very deeply. For some it is a long road from the head to the heart, but it is a journey that needs to be made. Feeling God's love is crucial to developing our spirituality. That is one reason why when I conduct directed retreats I ask the participants to spend a whole day allowing God to love them. They can do this in a variety of ways: praying over the scripture passages that deal with the topic; listening to songs or reading poetry on

God's love; spending time outdoors letting creation speak this message of love by contemplating a flower; and praying for people who have and continue to love us. This allows them to realize their love is only a spark of how much God loves them.

The more we feel God's love the more we will love ourselves and others. Saint Bernard once said that the hardest kind of love is to love oneself. This does not mean in a selfish way, but to recognize our goodness and go deeper into the well of that goodness, rather than being overly concerned about all our faults and shortcomings. One psychiatrist claimed that every psychosis he treated had its origin in the fact that the patient felt unlovable. He said that if he could convince clients they were personally loved by God, he would be out of business.

The reason why some Christians do not love others is because they don't love themselves. People they live or work with might point out all their faults or shortcomings and give them the impression that they are not lovable. God, however, continues to say I love you. Whom do we believe? Saints and faith-filled people are able to love others and themselves because they have felt deeply how much God loves them. When we feel deeply God's love we will not need a commandment to love others. We will realize that we are extensions of God's love to others. Much like a broken pitcher cannot hold water, often our shattered hearts can't seem to absorb God's love.

E. Ann Hillestad, a retired nurse, wrote, "Evangelization means sharing with another the irrefutable fact that God loves that person, regardless of how 'bad' he or she has been."[6] We need healing of our broken hearts, and as they heal our hearts will overflow with love. That certainly happened to Ferdinand Mahfood, who attributes his conversion in 1976 to realizing and feeling deeply how much God loved him. His organization, Food for the Poor, began shipping supplies to poverty-stricken people in 1982 and has shipped more than $433 million in food, medicine, and other supplies to thirty-three countries.[7]

Those who receive the baptism of the Spirit will often declare that it was at that moment they really felt loved by God. "For your love is better than wine" (Song 1:2) were the words read at a Bible meeting. These words suddenly were felt so deeply by a man at that meeting that they healed him of his alcoholism.

Father Rick Wendell, a priest of the archdiocese of Milwaukee, Wisconsin, had a near-death experience before becoming a priest. He cut himself in the neck during a landscaping project and needed stitches that were inserted without incident. However, the anesthesia caused him to go into cardiac arrest and the hospital personnel were unable to revive him initially. While unconscious he remembered seeing an intense light and later said, "I never knew I could be loved that much." He maintains that everything about his life after that experience changed, and eventually he became a priest at the age of forty-six.

Feeling God's love has an effect on so many aspects of our lives. We become willing to accept any suffering, hardships, trials, and difficulties more easily. We are not afraid to die. Some Christians maintain that they are not afraid of death, but dying is what they fear most. Woody Allen, the famous comedian and film director, said that he wasn't afraid of dying. He just does not want to be there when he dies.

What sustained Jesus in his passion and death was undoubtedly that he felt loved by the Father, even though he could say on the cross, "My God, my God, why have you forsaken me? (Matt 27:46).

A famous well-known speaker and evangelist who had been sharing the gospel for over fifty years was being interviewed. He was asked the question if there was anything he would change now after his fifty years of ministry to countless thousands of people. With an aged voice he responded: "If there was one thing that I could do over again, it would be to go back to every church, every meeting, every crusade, every individual, and instead of preaching the wrath and judgment of God, I would share his message of love and grace. That is what I failed to do and therefore regret most of all about my years of ministry." His name: Billy Graham. It took Billy Graham that long. Hopefully, we feel more deeply God's unconditional love for us much sooner. Once we do, we will be able to live with certainty in an uncertain and unstable world.

Saint John in his first epistle writes, "See what love the Father has given us, that we should be called children of God; and that is what we are. The reason the world does not know us is that it did not know him. Beloved, we are God's children now; what we shall be has not yet been Revealed" (1 John 3:1–2). What we shall come to realize and feel more deeply is how God is our lover, and that God's theme song is "Please remember me as loving you."

SCRIPTURE PASSAGES FOR REFLECTION

"Even these may forget, yet I will not forget you." (Isa 49:15)

"I have inscribed you on the palm of my hand." (Isa 49:16)

"I have loved you with an everlasting love." (Jer 31:3)

"O give thanks to the Lord for he is good, for his steadfast love endures forever." (Ps 136:1)

QUESTIONS TO CONSIDER

1. How can we accept the fact that God's love is personal and exclusive?

2. Why is God's love different from other loves?

3. How can we accept more the love that Jesus showed us?

4. Do we feel deeply how much God loves us and what can help us?

2

WHO IS MY NEIGHBOR?

"But wanting to justify himself, he asked Jesus:
'And who is my neighbor?'"
Luke 10:29

Once we have felt more deeply how much God loves us, we will then be able to reach out to others who are in much greater need. So to ask the question "Who is my neighbor" is far more important now than when the lawyer asked it of Jesus.

In Genesis, Cain asks, "Am I my brother's keeper?" (Gen 4:9). A similar question was asked of Jesus, and he told the well-known story of the Good Samaritan. The lawyer probably wanted a legal answer, but Jesus surprised him as well as all of his listeners. Maybe we need to surprise or challenge ourselves by asking the same question. If we study the fathers of the church as well as the scholastics, the story of the Good Samaritan was told as an allegory about Jesus. The man in the ditch signified Adam, who was expelled from the garden of Eden. The scribe and the priest who passed by represented the law and the prophets respectively. The stranger is Jesus, who anoints Adam and takes him to an inn that represents the church. Jesus returns in the Second Coming. So the neighbor is Jesus, who showed mercy. In this interpretation, we need to understand how we are challenged to imitate the neighbor and be a Good Samaritan.

As Father James F. Keenan, SJ, points out, "The parable, by being about Christ, is not first and foremost about what we are called to do. Rather, the parable is first and foremost about what Christ has done for us. This is key: we are the wounded man, and the Good Samaritan is the one who first has been merciful to us. Because we received his mercy, we are able to become merciful. In one and same parable we have the story of our salvation, and, then, the call to love our neighbor."[1]

Jesus challenges the lawyer in the Good Samaritan story not to name the neighbor but to become one. Who is the person in the ditch *now*? It could be anyone suffering from the various forms of violence in our society or in the world. To grasp better who is our neighbor we need to understand space, especially because we live in a mobile society and with much urban anonymity. As space increases so does our concept of neighbor. We are attempting to conquer outer space that is limitless, but we often fail to be aware of the space around us.

Traditionally, we considered neighbors as those who lived in our area or block. *Neighbor* in Greek means someone who lives nearby. However, many people don't even know who lives on the same block. I have visited homebound people and sometimes had to ask directions or inquire about where someone lived. In some instances, people didn't know that this person lived on their own block. We often know more about people living in Afghanistan, the Middle East, or elsewhere than we do about neighbors living in our locale. To extend the comparison, isn't it true that we know more about who are the contestants on *American Idol* or the characters on *The Simpsons*? How many of us can recite the Ten Commandments, know the seven sacraments, or even more challenging, the Beatitudes, which really indicate what kind of Christian we are?

We read or hear about belonging to a global village, but do we really know our global neighbors? America's refusal to sign the global warming treaty and land mine treaties, and its use of the island of Vieques as target practice even though the islanders consider us invaders, are indications we don't respect our neighbors. The Islamic cartoon controversy disproves the theory that the more knowledge we have of each other, the less prone we are to fight. We are learning that Muslims feel differently about the printed word, especially cartoons, and these differences have led to more violence.

Who then is our neighbor? In *Deus Caritas Est,* Pope Benedict XVI stated that up until the time of Jesus the concept of neighbor was understood as one's countrymen or foreigners who had settled in Israel. Today, this idea is too limited; now *neighbor* refers to anyone needing help.

Our neighbor is the innocent person on death row, the immigrants, the migrant farm worker trying to make a living on substandard wages, the millions of homeless, the senior citizens who have to make a choice between food and prescription drugs. Our neighbors are people we bypass today, especially those Judith Butler, a gender theorist, calls the "sexual abject," people who repel us by their sexual orientation and lifestyles.[2]

A good example of someone who was judged by sexual orientation is Matthew Shepherd, who was severely beaten and left to die on a fence post in Laramie, Wyoming. Other examples are people subjected to racism, sexism, sexual abuse, racial profiling, sexual predators, immigrants, trafficking (the United Nations Convention considers this the most serious violation of human rights), or people with AIDS or HIV virus. In the United States, twelve million children have parents who cannot afford the food needed to feed them. An eighteen-minute ride with nine stops in Manhattan will take a person from one of the richest neighborhoods to the poorest.

Did you ever notice how front porches are nonexistent in newly constructed homes? In one area people told the architects to construct their kitchens in the front, not in the rear, of the house so that they could more readily face the street and keep a watchful eye on their neighbors. At work, we rush around having little time to develop relationships. We do well interacting via the internet, but that is not eyeball to eyeball contact. How often do we read about, hear, or even experience rudeness or road rage in our society?

At mass we are asked to turn to our neighbor and offer some sign of greeting. But isn't there more needed? Pope Benedict XVI believes that the Eucharist is our opportunity to draw into Christ's most dynamic self-giving, where we become one with others. How welcoming are we as individuals or as a community?

Some parishes offer opportunities for fellowship like coffee and donuts, but what percentage attend those functions? How many parishes have the word *neighbor* in their mission statement? Some parishioners do take the message of being a neighbor seriously and volunteer their talents to rebuild homes in the poorer city areas.

Former president Jimmy Carter has set a powerful example in working for Habitat for Humanity. While doing this in the Philippines, the owner of a home noticed how Jimmy's sweat was dropping into the mortar of the home's foundation. Deeply impressed she said to him, "Now you are a part of us forever."[3]

Recently I read about a Father William Myrick of Christ Episcopal Church in Delavan, Wisconsin, who disguised himself as a homeless person. He begged for coins in front of his church where the mainly middle class seldom bump into poverty or stricken people. Most of the people avoided him; others walked silently past him as he sprawled out. A few contributed a total of twenty-three dollars. Some invited him in from the cold, but no one asked if he was ill. He later said, "I was getting angry seeing my friends pass me by. I realized it wouldn't take much and I could get in that same situation, and I couldn't count on those people." One parishioner commented, "The effect of it was probably one of the most profound things I've ever seen... I think it should be repeated at churches everywhere. It's enlightening to know how one reacts." Because of his deep concern, Myrick has rallied religious leaders and others to create an ecumenical shelter system in Walworth County, Wisconsin.

Mr. Rogers

The creator and host of *Mister Rogers' Neighborhood* told a story of the time he was on a vacation in New England. He attended a small church to hear a visiting preacher. He confessed that it was the worst sermon he ever heard. He thought to himself, "He has violated every principle of preaching, and this is a waste of time." Then he noticed a lady sitting next to him in tears. She said to him, "He said exactly what I need to hear." Fred Rogers then realized how judgmental he had been and how this message spoke to her heart because it was so personal.

What enabled Fred Rogers' career to last longer than many television stars who also directed their programs toward children? Other programs are certainly more sophisticated than his television show. The answer is that when Rogers spoke to children, he did not address them as "boys and girls," or someone out there in television land. He addressed them as "you." Even when singing, "Won't you be my neighbor," Rogers addressed the individual child and not just a group.[4]

This is certainly solid advice for us when we come into contact with others. How Christlike it is to treat them as important. People who are very successful in business know how vital personal and intimate language is. The personal approach that Mr.

Rogers did so well in his program insures engagement. How many of us are willing to interact that personally?

Strangers

In the Hebrew Scriptures, three groups needed to be shepherded: widows, orphans, and foreigners or strangers. We read in Leviticus that the Jews were told, "When an alien resides with you in your land, you shall not oppress the alien. The alien who resides with you shall be to you as the citizen among you; you shall love the alien as yourself, for you were aliens in the land of Egypt" (Lev 19:33–34).

Maybe many of our grandparents or great-grandparents "were once aliens" or strangers before coming to this country. Samaritans in the New Testament were certainly considered strangers, as demonstrated in the Good Samaritan story (Luke 10:25–37) and the healing of the ten lepers, when only one, a Samaritan, came back to thank Jesus (Luke 17:11–19). There is also the Samaritan woman who drew water at Jacob's well. After her exchange with Jesus, she invited others to believe in him (John 4:41). Notice in the Good Samaritan story, the lawyer is unable to say Samaritan but rather, "the one who showed him mercy" (Luke 10:37). The Jews held Samaritans in contempt and would not even speak to them on the streets. Peter insisted, however, once he encountered Cornelius "that God shows no partiality" (Acts 10:34).

Immigrants are certainly strangers in our country. Pope Benedict XVI noted that the migrant family should not be seen as a problem, but rather as a resource for humanity. Legal immigration is seen as a threat to American jobs, while illegal immigration raises the prospect of terrorism and crime. An injustice is involved in a failed immigration policy. Many immigrants cannot obtain jobs for which they are skilled and cannot get the insurance they deserve. Their children are unable to obtain financial aid that other American youth receive. Many immigrants live in constant fear of being discovered, being deported, and being separated from their families.

As Abraham Lincoln brought out in his proclamation of Thanksgiving Day (October 3, 1863), we as a nation are deeply indebted to immigrants. Up until recent times, they did not pose a threat to our nation. However, a drastic change has taken place, especially with immigrants from Asia and Latin America. We need to be aware of this problem and attempt to answer the questions: Are immigrants doing more harm than good? Are they taking away jobs from native-born Americans? How are they influencing our culture, politics, and way of life? Certainly these are ethical, legal, and biblical justice issues we need to address as Christians.

We encounter strangers in malls, bus and train stations, airports, shopping centers, and elsewhere. Ordinarily we don't engage in conversation. Is there something more expected of us besides ordinary courtesy? In another parable, Jesus stated that "When you give a luncheon or a dinner, do not invite your friends or your brothers or your relatives or rich neighbors, in case they invite you in return, and you would be repaid. But when you give a banquet, invite the poor, the crippled, the lame, the blind. And you will be blessed, because they cannot repay you, for you will be repaid at the resurrection of the righteous" (Luke 14:12–14). Whom do we invite? Saint Paul encouraged the Romans to "Contribute to the needs of the saints; extend hospitality to strangers" (Rom 12:13).

Susan Blum of Isaiah Ministries relates the experience of how their marriage encounter group of ten couples or more decided to do something on their own in a parish in Albany. At every Sunday mass, they found somebody they did not know and invited them to breakfast. After the initial shock of being invited, they were encouraged by the couples to do the same to others. Soon the whole parish knew each other.[5]

Tragedies Build Relationships

September 11, 2001, was indeed a tremendous tragedy that has been etched into our memories, especially for the people of New York City. However, it also transformed complete strangers into neighbors. Many heroic stories have been told of individuals willing to sacrifice their own lives to save others. People were willing to claw through endless wreckage hoping to find someone alive. Total strangers came to New York to help wherever they could.

Another story of heroism and unity tells how nine coal miners were saved in Somerset, Pennsylvania. One of the (maybe unsung) heroes was Joseph Shaffoni. He decided to rescue the miners by drilling a six-inch shaft down to the miners and forcing compressed air through it. That operation gave the miners air to breathe and kept the water at bay. Shaffoni also decided where to sink the shaft. The miners helped each other to the point that, if they were going to die or live, they would do it together.

In a similar way, Dr. Martin Luther King Jr. believed that we have to learn to live together otherwise we will die together. He saw how the world was becoming a neighborhood, but the greater challenge for Christians is to make it a brotherhood and sisterhood. We break down walls of mistrust and antagonism as soon as people become our neighbors. We are given new lenses to look at these people and appreciate who they really are in God's eyes, unconditionally loved.

For Christians there are no boundaries, borders, or limits. Learning this can be freeing and at the same time risky and dangerous. In the story of the Good Samaritan, the Levite and priest knew their boundaries and stayed in their safety zones. Not knowing if the man was dead, they did not want to touch a corpse because the Torah stated they would be unclean. Both of them were so occupied in obeying the law that they forgot how to be compassionate. Love must become more important than religious beliefs.

Our modern culture stresses how important our own goals are and tells us not to meddle in other people's affairs. Jesus makes it clear, "Just as you did it to one of the least of these who are members of my family, you did to me" (Matt 25:40). That approach and understanding removes all boundaries. Mother Teresa of Calcutta admitted that she saw God in the lepers she washed. She felt as if she were caring for Jesus. No boundaries, borders, or limits existed in her life as well as in so many who followed in her footsteps. She insisted that it was not a matter of how much we accomplished, but rather how much love was involved in doing it.

Love of God and Neighbor

Pope Benedict XVI in *Deus Caritas Est* insists that the love of God and love of neighbor are inseparable and the responsibility of every individual as well as the entire church. Karl Rahner, one of the eminent theologians of our time, also believes the love of God and neighbor are intimately connected. We have to admit how the majority of us live a peaceful coexistence or manage a surface relationship that often distances us from our neighbors. God intended us to find our fulfillment and freedom in reaching out to our neighbors. We find God when we are in communion with one another, and the opposite might also be true.

Rahner also shifts the love of neighbor to a deeper meaning of being in communion with all our brothers and sisters. This shift is certainly inspired by the Holy Spirit and reflects more the love of God and neighbor resulting in acts of service, kindness, compassion, and forbearance. Then love of neighbor ceases to be a command and enables us to be more Godlike.

Saint Paul wrote, "Owe no one anything, except to love one another; for the one who loves another has fulfilled the law" (Rom 13:8). Love becomes the beacon that shows the way. We have to learn not to substitute the good for the best in loving and helping others. Pope Benedict XVI explains in his first encyclical that the church is a network of charity reaching out especially to the poor. He believes that all civil and church institutions should be involved in alleviating economic, relational, and human poverty. That will mean at times practicing the highest type of love.

How often have we read or heard about soldiers in Iraq who are willing to throw themselves on a grenade to save their colleagues and are awarded a medal of honor? A book that I read, *The Greatest Gift,* about the inspiring life of Sister Dorothy Stang, a member of the Notre Dame de Namur religious community who was willing to return to Anapu, Brazil, to continue dedicating her life to land reform despite the possibility of being killed, reflects this spirit of giving one's life for the sake of others. Shortly after she returned, at the age of 73, she was brutally murdered on February 12, 2005. Stories such as these embody the words of Jesus who said, "No one has greater love than this, to lay down one's life for one's friends" (John 15:13).

The highest kind of love emphasized in the gospels consists in love that is not returned, love that has no or little reward, and love that is often accompanied by disappointment and ingratitude. Pope Benedict XVI believes that *agape,* the biblical notion of love, points to something new and distinct about our understanding of love. It is a love and concern for others putting aside all selfishness seeking the good of others. This love would empty our prisons, asylums, and hospitals. Waves of hatred and revenge beat in vain against the rock of true love. This love tests how heroic we are because we do not judge our brothers and sisters for their usefulness to us.

Rahner challenges us to *think* like Jesus, not in self-enclosed little boxes where we find ourselves at times, or ask ourselves, what would Jesus do? We can so easily get caught up in our own little world. Because this love is difficult for most of us, we might follow C. S. Lewis' advice in *Mere Christianity* to play the game of "Let's pretend," but the pretense has to lead to action.

Rahner also stresses the need to pray for others as another way to enter into deeper communion with all our brothers and sisters. Rahner was highly esteemed not only as a scholar but also because he practiced what he taught and preached. He cared for the poor and hungry and deeply felt the need for prayer in his own life. He believed that we need to change the expression "save your soul" to "save your neighbor."[6] What prevents us from helping others are the thousand little Lilliputian threads of rope that keep us in bondage so we are not really free. What also prevents us is what C. S. Lewis believed, that God didn't make us to be happy, but made us to love. If our goal in life is to be happy we will be miserable, but if our goal is to love we will be happy.

As Saint John points out, we cannot say we love God whom we do not see and hate our brother and sister whom we see (1 John 4:20). The God whom we do not see becomes visible in the neighbor we see. Jesus shared meals with sinners and tax collectors and was accused of doing so by the scribes and Pharisees (Mark 2:16). Communion with these outcasts was a much higher value for Jesus than the law.

Saint Paul stated concerning the body, "if one member suffers, all suffer together with it" (1 Cor 12:26). This can easily be applied to all the suffering in the world at the present time as well as our ecology and other areas of injustice. An African saying expresses the idea of relationship well: "I exist because we all do, therefore, I am." Martin Buber's *I and Thou* certainly emphasizes the need for us to relate in meaningful ways. Even our bodies are composed of billions of cells, and, according to biologists, they are communicating with each other.

Love of Self and Neighbor

A scholar of the law asked Jesus what was the greatest commandment. He responded: "You shall love the Lord your God with all your heart, and with all your soul, and with all your mind. This is the greatest and the first commandment. And a second is like it: You shall love your neighbor as yourself" (Matt 22:36–39).

Loving God and others with all our hearts, minds, and strength means stretching them to their limits. Then God can more readily take up residence in our hearts. God loves dwelling not in small hearts but palatial ones. Jesus' love is the plumb line by which everything should be measured. True love is more demanding than laws, and that is why Jesus challenged us to show the highest kind of love. What often prevents this from occurring is our inability to accept the faults of others that are in many instances our own faults. If this is true, it explains why we so readily are able to detect their faults. Christ's love sees others with a telescope, not a microscope. We also need a telescope to realize that after two thousand years of spreading the gospel message, only a third of the human population identify themselves as Christians.

The risen Christ tells Thomas, "Enter my wounds." Caravaggio's famous painting depicts Thomas looking curiously into the wounds. Yes, we need to enter the wounds of the world and our nation, the wounds of our neighbors, but to do so with the love Jesus asked of Peter, "Do you love more than these?" (John 21:15). That question probes the conscience of any Christian and move us into action so we can love others more than our computers, cell phones, and cars. We become more attached to the latter than the former, especially the weak and powerless who often act as mirrors of our inner souls.

We might insist that we get rid of the street people because then we will not see their wounds. Actually what we fear more are our fragile, weak, vulnerable, wounded selves. Maybe "touching" Christ's wounds will help us to touch the untouchable. Christians have to be ready to descend the security of Mount Tabor, and be ready to enter the garden of Gethsemane and then mount the cross of Christ.

Buddhists insist that love of self and love of neighbor are equal. In their philosophy, all unhappiness stems from desiring happiness for ourselves only. We can blame most everything on being preoccupied with oneself, but the focus has to be on others. Buddhists go so far as to suggest breathing in others' suffering, and breathing out love, compassion, and care.

The prophet Mohammed singled out who are our neighbors: people forty houses in front of us, in back of us, and on the side of us. He was once asked about a woman who fasted, prayed, and gave to charitable causes, but was very uncharitable in speech to her neighbor. He responded that she is in hell fire. Similarly, Shane Clairborne in *The Irresistible Revolution* suggests that most middle-class Christians are not doing enough, despite the fact that here in our country $295 billion is given in charitable contributions annually.

Our contribution or our act of kindness does not have to be as earth shaking as the following story of a man who showed concern for others. His house contained vermin. He called the pest control company and found out that they could get rid of the vermin. However, when the man found out the vermin would leave his house and go somewhere else in the neighborhood, he said no. How many of us would have acted in a similar way?

Dietrich Bonhoeffer preached very forcefully on the topic of love of neighbor, insisting that this was the hallmark of being a disciple of Jesus, who proved himself our neighbor by dying on the cross. He was critical of the German churches that had avoided concrete action to overcome the evils of the Nazis.

In John's Gospel, Jesus prayed for himself, his disciples, and for all believers so "that they may all be one" (John 17:21). This prayer has not been answered yet and will only come to fruition when we love our neighbor as ourselves. Our coins carry the motto *E Pluribus Unum,* "From the many, one." Yet, that remains our challenge as Christians.

Tertullian reported to the pagans that when the Christians came out of their meetings, he noticed how they loved each other. His famous expression concerning Christians is found in his *Apologeticum* (ch 39, 7): "Look how they love one another." What do others say about Christians today? Jesus said, "By this everyone will know that you are my disciples, if you have love for one another" (John 13:35). Sometimes in loving others or being loved we are going to be burned or jilted, as the saying goes. Our natural tendency is to refuse to love or be loved like that again. However, it is better to have loved and not succeeded than not to have loved at all. The highest kind of love continues to love and be loved.

We need to approach the Good Samaritan story as if we are reading or hearing it for the first time. We have to imagine how this story sounded to Jesus' listeners when they heard it for the first time. Our problem often is that we know the story too well. How do we distance ourselves from the story?

A parable like this one and others often leaves questions unanswered and open to many possibilities, especially the shock value. Another way is to read the text aloud very slowly, dwelling and reflecting upon the words. Maybe a word, phrase, or a sentence will stand out. We might be surprised what happens. What made the Samaritan stop and help the man? Pity, compassion, or was he himself an outcast? Why would Jesus choose a Samaritan as hero of the story? Was it the bitter rivalry between the Jews and Samaritans? Do we notice how Jesus really does not answer the lawyer's question by defining who a neighbor is? Jesus clarified that the lawyer is a neighbor when he acts like the Good Samaritan that implies risk and exposure to vulnerability. Someday we hope to arrive at a point where as Good Samaritans we consider it a privileged responsibility to care for people in hospitals, nursing homes, hospices, and prisons, and the homeless.

Larry Stewart was convinced that we are here on this earth to help others. Known as the Secret Santa, he spent every December for twenty-six years giving away money roaming the streets of Kansas City, Missouri, and elsewhere. He died of cancer in January 2007 at the age of 58, having given away more than one million dollars. He did it without being found out until near the end of his life.[7]

There is a short story about Mother Teresa of Calcutta that one day a man came to her saying there was a family of eight children who had not eaten for days. She immediately took some food and went to the family, where she saw the disfigured faces of the children but no sadness, just deep pain. She gave the food to the mother, who distributed some of the food to the children and then left. When she returned, the mother was asked where she had gone; she responded, "To my neighbors—they are hungry too." Remember how Jesus concluded the story, "Go, and do likewise" (Luke 10:37).

❈   ❈   ❈

SCRIPTURE PASSAGES FOR REFLECTION

"Do not plan harm against your neighbor who lives trustingly beside you." (Prov 3:29)

"Those who despise their neighbors are sinners, but happy are those who are kind to the poor." (Prov 14:21)

"We who are strong ought to put up with the feelings of the weak, and not please ourselves. Each of us must please our neighbor for the good purpose of building up the neighbor." (Rom 15:1–2)

"Let mutual love continue. Do not neglect to show hospitality to strangers." (Heb 13:1)

QUESTIONS TO CONSIDER

1. Who are the outcasts of our society that we avoid?

2. Why do we watch our neighbors but fear involvement?

3. Are there instances that we acted as Good Samaritans?

4. What prevents us from accepting the faults of others when they often are our own faults?

5. What are the Lilliputian ropes that keep us in bondage?

3

HOW DISCIPLINED ARE YOU?

"Endure your trials for the sake of discipline."
Heb 12:7

Do we follow Jesus' advice, "Go and do likewise?" To accomplish this daunting task we need to examine ourselves by asking the question: How disciplined am I? How many disciplined Christians do you know?

Webster's Dictionary defines discipline as a "training that corrects, molds, or perfects the mental faculties or moral character; [it is] an orderly or prescribed conduct or pattern of behavior, a self-control." We need to evaluate that definition and become more aware of some of the elements that make up discipline. It definitely is a pattern of behavior or a self-control needed by Christians if we are to grow in our spiritual as well as our physical, emotional, and psychological lives.

Anthony deMello maintained that if something within us urges us in the right direction, it creates its own discipline. Discipline, however, is not reserved to ascetic and contemplative Christians; God intended discipline for all of us.

We live in a creature comfort society where we are strongly attracted to self-gratification. If we are hungry, we eat. If we feel lazy, we idle away our time or procrastinate. If we feel like smoking or drinking to excess, we do so without considering the consequences. Because we live in a society with instant coffee, tea, low interest rates, and a host of other instant gratifications, we long to have things at our fingertips and get upset when they aren't functioning properly.

Disciplined people, however, know how to act in this creature comfort world. Their self-control enables them to follow a prescribed way of conducting themselves or pattern of behavior. They have the wisdom to understand and appreciate discipline as in Proverbs 1:2, where discipline is used to dispel ignorance and correct vice.

Discipline can also be viewed as delayed satisfaction, often the essence of discipline. Its purpose is to help us change, convert, or transform our vision or perception. The Letter to the Hebrews says: "In your struggle against sin you have not yet resisted to the point of shedding blood. And you have forgotten the exhortation that addresses you as children—My child, do not regard lightly the discipline of the Lord or lose heart when you are punished by him; for the Lord disciplines those whom he loves, and chastises every child whom he loves" (Heb 12:4–6). Yet how many of us enjoy the discipline of a divine parent or any parent? During trying circumstances or difficult challenges, we are given an opportunity to discipline ourselves and grow knowing that God does not abandon us, as we read in the Second Book of the Maccabees, "Although he disciplines us with calamities, he does not forsake his own people" (2 Mac 6:16).

This delayed satisfaction received while disciplining ourselves becomes evident in the field of sports. Baseball, football, basketball, swimming, and other sports demand much practice and grueling exercise. Most professional football players will admit that they despise training camp while getting themselves in shape.

Olympic competitors spend as much as seven hours a day practicing for an event. Some of these events last a few minutes, but the satisfaction of winning a medal, the World Series, or the Super Bowl cannot compare to the exhausting hours of preparation.

Apolo Anton Ohno provides a good example. He won a gold medal in the men's 500-meter event in short track speed skating in the 2006 Olympics. To accomplish this feat, he spent much time in seclusion, disciplining himself for this important venture in his life. Saint Paul wrote, "I punish my body and enslave it, so that after proclaiming to others I myself should be disqualified" (1 Cor 9:27).

The same kind of discipline is needed in other areas, such as music. Anyone wishing to become proficient or professional will have to spend hours practicing each day. Archbishop Rembert Weakland, the former archbishop of Milwaukee, Wisconsin, noticed when he was a student at Juliard Academy how many gifted students with innate talent were there. He also noticed how many would not succeed because they did not discipline themselves to perform well but wasted their talents and outstanding abilities.

Japan seems to have a stronger type of discipline in comparison with the United States. Children are prepared to test their limits in all fields, including music. Western music came to Japan after World War II and became part and parcel of their lives. Students of violin discipline themselves by practicing eight to ten hours a day. Isaac Stern, the famous violinist who has a gusto for life and a passion for working with younger musicians, maintains that Japan has a stronger discipline than the United States. Lang Lang, who grew up in Shenyang, China, is an example of a pianist who at the age of nine was told by his teacher, "You will never be a pianist." However, his father, Guo-ren Lang, believed in him and told him "You'd better practice." He continued to discipline himself by practicing for hours each day and has played with the Chicago Symphony Orchestra, at the Lincoln Center, and at Carnegie Hall.

If we want discipline, the Book of Wisdom makes it very clear what the first step is, "The beginning of wisdom is the most sincere desire for instruction," which is discipline (Wis 6:17). So we have to ask ourselves, do we really desire discipline and see how it can help us to love more? No endeavor in life can succeed without some form of discipline, especially our seeking for a deeper relationship with God (Sir 32:14). John Shea, a theologian and story-teller, writes that the mind makes a good servant but a poor master. Turning it into a servant, however, certainly requires discipline.

One of the tasks of some of the prophets was to help the Jewish people to discipline themselves as they awaited their return from the exile. Ezra and Nehemiah enkindled their hope by developing a strong liturgy for the Jews. Jeremiah pointed out to the people that they had not accepted the Lord's discipline, and as a result truth had perished (Jer 7:8).

Jesus, the greatest prophet of all, was most disciplined. Shortly before the passage on discipline in the Letter to the Hebrews the author advises us to look "to Jesus the pioneer and perfecter of our faith, who for the sake of the joy that was set before him he endured the cross, disregarding its shame, and has taken his seat at the right hand of the throne of God" (Heb 12:2). He was willing to suffer, die, and rise to new life, and he invites us to do the same. His crucifixion can never compare to any of our suffering. He endured the most ignominious death on a cross, as the author in Deuteronomy states: "Anyone hung on a tree is under God's curse" (Deut 21:23). The corpse was not to remain on the tree overnight, but had to be buried the same day, otherwise God's curse would rest on it.

Saint Paul refers to this when he writes: "Christ redeemed us from the curse of the law by becoming a curse for us" (Gal 3:13).

This delayed satisfaction that Jesus received, however, cannot compare to his intense suffering, pain, and crucifixion. Saint Paul tells us: "Therefore God highly exalted him and gave him the name that is above every name, so that at the name of Jesus every knee should bend, in heaven and on earth, and under the earth, and every tongue should confess that Jesus is Lord, to the glory of God the Father" (Phil 2:9–11).

Willingness to Pay the Price

Many Christians don't want to pay the price of pain before receiving the delayed satisfaction. Yet this is the cost of discipleship. Discipline and discipleship are closely allied. Pain is involved in going on a diet, cutting down or stopping our excessive smoking or drinking, watching less television, or not spending so much time playing games on a computer.

We often experience similar pain in going to a store and seeing something that we like. As we pick up the item, the first thing we do is look at the price tag. Have you ever noticed how small the price tag is? My mother would ask me how much an article costs because she could not read it. If it costs too much we immediately put it back. Disciplining oneself in these and similar areas is comparable to a spiritual sauna bath.

Jesus was willing to pay the price with his blood. At the Last Supper he said to his disciples as he passed them a cup: "This is my blood of the covenant, which is poured out for many" (Mark 14:24). As the soldier pierced his lance into Jesus' side, Saint John tells us "And at once blood and water came out" (John 19:34).

An expression often used is that there is "no gain without some pain." However, our society seemingly does not want us to experience any pain or suffering. The commercial for Advil tells us, "I haven't got the time for the pain." Despite all our medical advances, we are still baffled because we can't escape suffering and pain. In fact, we have miracle drugs, organ transplants, pacemakers, artificial hearts, bionic eyes, advances in psychotherapy and social science, but we still have not found a cure for the common cold. Other forms of suffering and pain are a result of our increased leisure time: boredom, monotony, or routine. We can feel a sense of automation in our work that increases our hopelessness and powerlessness.

Some of us try to escape suffering and pain by denying it. We consider it a social taboo. Some don't want to consider what happens to others: the parents of a three-year-old child racked with pain, the husband or wife who just lost a job, the teenager killed in a tragic car accident. We would rather keep suffering and pain at arm's length, see it a safe distance on our television screen or in a movie theater.

The disciplined person is willing to face and embrace suffering no matter how difficult an ordeal involved. For example, Buddhists work tirelessly to discipline themselves in letting go of all selfish desires. Proverbs 5:23 says that we will die from lack of discipline or even be lost. However, disciplined people accept this imposing challenge, especially when facing ordeals. What is the difference in people who, when they lose a job or home, find out that they have Alzheimer's or cancer, find that their lives are shattered, whereas others become stronger through these adversities? The latter put their faith in God and not in institutions or themselves. God becomes their anchor and safety when the waters get rough.

Some time ago a mother told me about her thirteen miscarriages. I was astounded to hear this. She struggled to accept the weakness of these setbacks in her life and spent a long time reconciling herself to God. Fortunately, she did, but many don't.

Advanced Decision Making

Another important element in disciplining ourselves is to make our decision in advance. Jesus made his decision to go up to Jerusalem to suffer, die, and then rise. Nothing deterred him from his decision or resolve, despite the temptations he received. Saint Luke tells us in his Gospel, "Jesus, full of the Holy Spirit returned from the Jordan and was led by the Spirit in the wilderness, where for forty days he was tempted by the devil" (Luke 4:1–2) The devil knew Jesus' strength but he wanted to find his weakness.

Everyone has an Achilles' heel. Adam's weakness was found in Eve. Moses' patience was tested by the rebellious Israelites. David's weakness was exposed by the ravishing beauty of a woman named Bathsheba. Was Jesus, the human being, any different? The devil had to find out!

The first temptation offered by the devil was for Jesus to change a stone into a loaf of bread. Jesus makes it very clear that we don't live on bread alone. This temptation is commonly interpreted as a craving for material things.[1] Our society places a heavy emphasis on material goods, which become for many an all-absorbing interest and goal. Youth today describe their reaction to our way of life as "society's soulless materialism," yet many of them fall into the same trap of materialism by buying the best clothes, shoes, and other goods.

Karl Rahner, the famous German theologian, refers to seeking after material goods as a subtle heresy. Just as materialism is our heresy, the early church struggled with philosophies that would take people away from Christ. They faced many heresies, among them the Arian heresy that denied the divinity of Christ. It was spreading so rapidly that Saint Jerome feared that one day the church would wake up and find itself Arian. Today, materialism is far more subtle and creeps into our lives and saps imperceptibly our spiritual energy.

Saint Francis of Assisi was so well aware of the materialism of his time that he performed a radical act: he renounced all material things and committed his life to Gospel poverty. Even Bishop Guido urged Francis to accept money, but he said no. Francis didn't want anyone poorer than himself. Murray Bodo writes, "I do not think that Francis was a social reformer who saw what money would do to the fabric of society. He was rather the quintessential Christian who saw what money would do to the spirit."[2] His radical act took much discipline.

Craving after material things, like so many other things, can squeeze the juice out of our lives. The result is that we become like shriveled up orange peels. Material goods become dangerous when they turn us away from God, making us more independent and more trusting in ourselves alone. Or they can lead to unjust practices of graft, cheating, and stealing, so prevalent in our society. "Live simply that others might live" has inspired many to give up many material goods, waste nothing, and promote simplicity.[3]

The pie is not large enough to feed everyone. We need to make important choices: the food we eat; the clothing we wear; how we utilize energy; where we shop; how, where, and what we drive; recycling. The decisions we make will have an impact on the entire planet and its inhabitants.

Imagine the impact Christian leaders could have on others if they modeled a simple life style. Our lifestyle drives us to become busier and busier. Only when we taste a simple life style will we grasp how frantic we have become. The more we strive after a frenzied lifestyle the less time we have for living. If we spend eight hours at a job and the evening watching television, how can we have time for personal relationships?

Consumerism

Consumerism enslaves rather than liberates. We need to expose the lie and illusion that it liberates and leads to happiness. The apparent satisfaction leads to dissatisfaction and lack of fulfillment. Consuming less will lead to real happiness and fulfillment. Our desire for material things is shown by our drive to buy things not really needed. The disciplined person makes a distinction between real needs and unnecessary wants.

Some of us tie ourselves into economical knots because we haven't conquered the consumerism so rampant in our society. Our main concern is what are we going to buy next, rather than how can we simplify our lifestyle. We want to live in the lap of luxury, but we pay the price by becoming workaholics. The magazine *Adbusters* advocates that on the day after Thanksgiving, which is always a countrywide shopping frenzy, people instead buy nothing at all. The "ad" pictures Jesus saying, "I never told you to buy *everyone* a Christmas gift for my birthday." But we need more than one day to counteract our overconsumption.[4]

Consumerism stresses three main points:

1. Products are more important than religion.
2. Products are more important than people.
3. Products are substitutes for deeper human needs.

Who needs God when you have a MasterCard® or an unlimited expense account? Consumerism enslaves rather than liberates. An adequate supply of life's necessities will lead to healthier relationships and happiness. As Christians we need to disempower the forces promoting and profiting from consumerism.

Parents often make the mistake of giving their children many material things. Some call it the miracle of the pocketbook, enabling parents to keep children quiet and obedient. The rationalization is that their children will be better off than they were. However, children today need parents who take time to listen, love, support, affirm, and discipline them. As the Book of Proverbs exhorts: "Discipline your children while there is hope" (Prov 19:18). That means to provide direction and correction when necessary. The main purpose of correction is not to punish but to train children. Well-disciplined children are a boon to their parents. The opposite is true: "Pamper a child, and he will terrorize you; play with him and he will grieve you" (Sir 30:9).

Lance Morrow wrote an article in *Time* about William Bennett's best seller *The Book of Virtues* stating that the book should be a companion to or used as an owner's manual by parents. Bennett states that virtue demands discipline and self-abnegation, but we live in an age where discipline and self-abnegation are not priorities in reaching our goals.[5]

Power

The devil tempted Jesus a second time when Jesus was on top of a high mountain with a panoramic view of everything. The devil offers him all this power and glory. Jesus responds that it is the Lord God you shall adore and give homage. One form of power is money. Money is power and prestige. Paul Getty, a very wealthy man, was asked to write his autobiography. He wrote it in just a few words: I became a billionaire. What a contrast to a lady whom I met a few years ago. She had many fond memories of her deceased husband. She always treasured one catchy statement: "Honey, we don't have a lot of money, but we have a lot of love."

Jesus made it very clear that "No one can serve two masters... You cannot serve God and wealth" (Matt 6:24). Notice that only wealth or money is put on a par with God, not reputation, family, talents, or knowledge. In the gospels, next to the reign of God, what do you think Jesus talked most about? Money!

The first letter of Timothy tells us, "For the love of money is a root of all kinds of evil" (1Tim 6:10). Many have drunk the poisonous potions of this kind of power that leads to destruction. In the Hebrew Scriptures, we read of Delilah who betrayed Samson for money. Judas sold Jesus for thirty pieces of silver. Since then many have sold Christ across the counter for their dishonest practices. How many have worshiped at the altar of money, power, success, and control?

Craving after money can become a god in our lives. Marx called money our "jealous god." How do we create these self-made gods? Our God can be any value to which we give highest place in our lives. This will often be revealed to us in time of searing struggles or when choosing between two values. This value can be work, health, money, drink, immoral sex, or anything that controls us. It takes much discipline to make the right choice or decision. Jesus put it succinctly: "For where your treasure is, there your heart will be also" (Matt 6:21). What do you think of most? Where are your thoughts centered? There is your heart.

Jesus resisted the temptation of power to accomplish his mission. He fulfilled his mission by suffering, dying, and rising. Jesus did not seek exploitative and manipulative power over others that many of us use today. He disciplined himself by exercising his power over sickness, illness, disease, and death. The devil wanted Jesus to exert a temporary power, like a meteor streaking across the sky but burning itself out before reaching the earth.

From the very beginning, human beings have been seduced by power. Adam and Eve experienced this in the serpent's temptation to be "like God." Ever since that time power has been disguised to tempt us. For example, the Puritans maintained that they could judge anyone's faithfulness to God by how prosperous or wealthy they were. Striving for wealth then became a priority in their lives and led to the abuse of power over others. As Christians, we need to make sure that we live under God's power, which can bring order out of chaos, redeem us from the slavery of sin, and help us to care for all people, especially the poor and marginalized.

Sensationalism

His third temptation found Jesus on the pinnacle of the temple and the devil asking him to throw himself down and allow the angels to catch him before he hit the ground. This might be interpreted as a clever temptation to sensationalism.

Many of us have an inborn desire to do something sensational or outstanding, to make a name for ourselves. In Genesis we read: "Come, let us build ourselves a city, and a tower with its top in the heavens, and let us make a name for ourselves; otherwise we shall be scattered abroad upon the face of the whole earth" (Gen 11:4). We know what happened to the people who tried to build the tower of Babel. They were scattered, alienated, estranged. We have no need to build a name for ourselves if we discipline ourselves to reflect often on how much God loves us. God loves us for what we are and can become.

Very few of us will accomplish outstanding deeds. Our names are not going to splash across newspaper headlines, our successes will not be blurted out over the media as news of the moment. Tuesday is a dull echo of Monday, and Thursday a faint carbon copy of Wednesday. And by the time we get to Friday, we say, "Thank God, it is Friday." So there is a need to make a decision to live our ordinary lives like Jesus did; only three years of his life were spent in public ministry.

As Mother Teresa of Calcutta maintained: "It is not how successful we are in life, but how faithful we are to God." Being faithful to our ordinary tasks requires much discipline. I asked an elderly sister how long she had taught in grade school. She replied, "Fifty years." Now that takes discipline and dedication. Florence Verstynen of Norfolk, Virginia, has been a crossing guard for nearly fifty years. She exclaimed that she would not want to be in any other place. Andy Warhol, the famous painter and film maker, said that "in the future, everyone will be famous for fifteen minutes." For many people, like Florence Verstynen, even that is too long.

The three temptations of Jesus are our temptations. The constant temptation that Jesus had throughout his life was to accomplish his mission in some other way than by suffering, dying, and rising. His final temptation came on the cross when the people scoffed and mocked him saying, "He saved others; let him save himself if he is the Messiah of God, his chosen one" (Luke 23:35). He was faithful to the end because he disciplined himself to overcome his threefold temptation. Can we do the same?

Accountability

Another element of discipline is accountability. Jesus made it very clear how he was accountable to his loving Father. He committed himself to do whatever the Father wanted him to accomplish. When Jesus was found in the temple by Mary and Joseph, he told them that he had to be about his Father's business. He went back with them to Nazareth and was subject to them—God subject to human beings! He came to do his Father's will and not his own (John 8:40). His goal was to do the Father's will (John 4:34). He was willing to lay down his life freely (John 10: 7–18).

Only someone who had disciplined himself throughout his life was able to accomplish all that.

We need to ask ourselves often how committed we are. Jesus showed how it was possible to give oneself completely by totally involving himself with others. Gabriel Marcel, a twentieth-century French existentialist philosopher, maintained that we can know ourselves only to the extent we commit ourselves to others. Many of us are committed to our work, job, or other tasks, but fail to share ourselves with others. The former is often described as constancy, the latter as commitment. Scott Peck, a famous psychiatrist, states that commitment is at the rock foundation of any truly loving relationship. To foster that kind of commitment takes much discipline.

There are three things to think about:

1. From where did we come?
2. To where we are going?
3. To whom must we give an account?

Rendering an account in a responsible adult way for our decisions and actions can be most challenging, especially when we take the initiative. We often need to risk doing new and innovative things. If we happen to outrun others, then we have to wait as John waited for Peter to arrive at the tomb on resurrection day. Disciplined people are not satisfied doing only what they have to accomplish but are constantly looking for new horizons.

Michael Timmis, who serves on the National Fellowship of Men, relates how he was asked to share what being converted to Jesus Christ meant in his life. He was invited by many groups to tell about this experience. Being a businessman, he was reminded by a friend that people were watching him to see if he was for real. His friend also told him that if he fell others would fall with him. Timmis admitted what helped him not to let down Jesus Christ was disciplining himself.[6]

Freedom

Disciplined people are truly free. We often have the wrong attitude toward our freedom. It is not a question of doing as we like, but doing as we ought. It is not like the bumper sticker that reads: "If it feels good, do it." Or Saint Augustine's expression that all you have to do is love and do what you want. The emphasis needs to be placed on the first part, not the last part.

Peter Gillquist, an Orthodox archpriest, summarizes the idea of personal choice: "We have become a nation of self-lovers. Nothing is too sacred to leave—if we feel like it. We leave school if it gets boring or difficult; we leave home and parents if we're displeased; we leave our jobs, our marriages, and our churches."[7] We pick and choose as quickly as we change our television channels or brands found in the supermarket. We are free to the degree we commit ourselves to God in total dependence.

Jesus was the most free person because he embodied this paradox. Jesus assured us that the truth will make us free. Pilate could ask Jesus, "What is truth?" failing to grasp that truth itself was standing in front of him (John 18:38). If a disciplined person is one who shows self-control, Jesus demonstrated it well before Pilate.

Necessary for Spiritual Development

Discipline of one's mind and body are absolutely necessary if we are going to develop our spiritual lives. To become holy we need to discipline ourselves because the aim of all spirituality is union with God. It takes much discipline not to let anything interfere with that goal. Often what can interfere are our moods.

Moody people often find it hard to grow deeply in their spiritual lives because they have not disciplined themselves to control their moods. Moody behavior can be a sign of inferiority, a deep hurt caused by someone, or something else troubling the person. Sooner or later, if we have not already, we will come in contact with moody people. The disciplined person does not allow moody people to ruin his or her day. Being pleasant and kind to them, especially by lending a listening ear, demands much discipline. The hard part is not allowing someone else to beat you in loving them.

Rick Warren has written *The Purpose Driven Life,* a compelling, challenging book about our purpose on earth and our spiritual goal in life. He calls the book a forty-day spiritual journey. It all starts with God, and we are no accidents. Warren asks, what drives our life? We need to view life from God's perspective, that life is only temporary leading to eternal life. Our lives need to be based on God's purposes and not on our worldly or cultural values that lead to stress, frustration, depression, and meaninglessness. To maintain such a spiritual goal and purpose demands much discipline.

Discipline is not an end in itself but a means to an end. If being a follower or disciple of Jesus means to discipline ourselves, then Jesus assures us: "A disciple is not above the teacher, but everyone who is fully qualified will be like the teacher" (Luke 6:40). What a marvelous promise to a Christian!

☀ ☀ ☀

SCRIPTURE PASSAGES FOR REFLECTION

"Do not regard lightly the discipline of the Lord, or lose heart
when you are punished;
for the Lord disciplines those whom he loves." (Heb. 12:5–6)

"Endure your trials for the sake of discipline." (Heb. 12:7)

"All discipline seems painful rather than pleasant at the time, but
later it yields the peaceful fruit of righteousness to those who
have been trained by it." (Heb. 12:11)

"Athletes exercise self-control in all things; they do it to receive a
perishable wreath, but we an imperishable one." (1 Cor. 7:25)

QUESTIONS TO CONSIDER

1. How much self-control do we have, or do we consider
   ourselves a disciplined person?

2. Are we willing to pay the price of the pain or suffering
   involved when disciplining ourselves?

3. Have we fallen into the trap of materialism or
   consumerism, or do we try to live simply?

4. Has money or something else become our "jealous god"?

5. Are we faithful in performing small tasks?

4

GOING BEYOND
TOLERANCE

*"Love your enemies, do good to those who hate you, bless those who
curse you, pray for those who abuse you."*
Luke 6:27–28

Disciplining ourselves as Christians will prepare us to move
beyond tolerance. To stand up against "the hammer of popular acclaim," to assert one's freedom against suffocating intolerance, false ideologies, and mob violence, is indeed a worthy cause
for Christians. If done with love, justice, and discipline, we will
certainly lose friends as Albert Camus, Simone Weil, and especially Jesus, did.

Webster's Dictionary's second definition of tolerance is "sym-
pathy or indulgence for beliefs or practices differing from or conflicting with one's own." At first blush, tolerance seems a good
way to help build community and wholesome relationships. It
means accepting people, the faithful as well as the faithless,
flawed yet possessing much potential, weak and at the same time
strong. To live that as Christians is challenging.

Tolerance implies a state of equality, a state of agreement, or
a state of truce and peace. Degrees of tolerance exist. Utter tolerance means anything goes, and when that happens, everything

goes. Mere tolerance means that individuals do not take their belief system very seriously and often leave their faith unattended. Their approach is that all of us are in different boats headed for the same shore. But are we? Many of us are not redeemed, and others have a laissez-faire approach to their faith.

Helen Keller believed that tolerance required the same effort as trying to ride a bike. Does tolerance mean putting up with people we find obnoxious and boisterous, or immigrants with strange customs, or not making judgments of others even in our hearts? As Christians we are called to a deeper unity and love than mere tolerance, as Pope Benedict XVI points out in *Deus Caritas Est*. If we are falsely accused or hurt we have a tendency to blame and complain about those who have done this to us. When we, however, hurt or blame others, God does not blame us or complain, but extends God's unconditional love to us.

Few of us will deny that we are a culture of blame and revenge, especially toward Islamic people since the September 11th tragedy. In reaction to the riots following his brutal beating, Rodney King expressed it well when he asked, "Can't we all get along?" We have to go beyond just getting along or tolerating each other. Tolerance might be able to keep us in relationship with one another, but it does not reconcile us with our sisters and brothers when necessary.

Tolerance is better than intolerance, biases, prejudices, looking down on others, or using hate-filled language or actions. The Internet has been tarnished by Web sites that spread hate. They can reach into the room of any child who has a computer and disguise their messages in deceptive ways. Hate crimes have increased since the Roman persecution of Christians to the Holocaust, the "ethnic cleansing" in Bosnia, the genocide in Rwanda, as well as the hatred here in the United States. The dragging death of James Byrd Jr. in Jasper, Texas, is an example. Despite the progress of integrated schools, unequal treatment and stereotypes of minorities still exist. As Christians we need to fight all forms of hate, pushing them out of our communities.

We have to become more aware of our prejudices, biases, and discrimination, which are often a sign of insecurity, and allow ourselves to be confronted if necessary. Such a viewpoint and understanding demands much humility. Some of us are not aware how prejudiced we are to another race or nationality.

How many of us can readily admit that we are racists? Newspapers, magazines, television, advertising, and movies definitely have an influence on our behavior. A trade journal of 1915 described motion pictures as "the world's pulpit." Is that true today?

Tolerance has its limits and it is only a first step toward understanding and cooperation. As we struggle with sexism, racism, homophobia, different cultures and religions, tolerance is one of the ways to help transform and change our lives. We might have a tendency to deny our biases and prejudices, and maintain we do not discriminate. Do we, however, respect people of other religious faiths?

Karl Barth considered people of other faiths as "lesser lights"; Paul Tillich called them "Christians incognito"; and Karl Rahner referred to them as "anonymous Christians" who could be saved. Are there scriptural passages which are exclusionary or discriminatory? Do we listen attentively to others who share a different faith or viewpoint, especially when these lead to much anger and harsh statements?

Understanding Religious Traditions

As Christians, we need to stretch our thinking to a better understanding of religious traditions that implies compassion, encouragement, and comfort. Oprah Winfrey encourages others to think about things differently. Maybe we need to alert ourselves to how important it is to develop a new theology of religion because religions differ as much as cultures.

One teacher of comparative religions takes her students to Hindu temples, Sikh gurdwaras, and Islamic centers. Recently, I read a book on the Islam religion and it gave me a whole different insight into their beliefs. Pope Paul VI in *Ecclesiam Suam* (1964) suggested that religious freedom should be a theme for interreligious dialogue that might prevent major collisions between various religious groups. Since Vatican II we have recognized Protestants as graced communities, but are we as tolerant of our immigrants? Are we aware of the drastic changes that have taken place in our religious landscape?

Diana L. Eck maintains in *A New Religious America* that we have become the most religiously diverse nation on this earth. So the questions arise: How much diversity is too much? How much religious freedom do we allow with our religious differences? Do we kill those who speak a different language or proclaim a different religion? Much damage has been done by religious leaders like Jerry Falwell, a Religious Right spokesperson, who condemned Islam and called Mohammed a terrorist, and declared that homosexuals, liberals, and feminists were responsible for the September 11th tragedy. How often Jews and Muslims, Hindus and Muslims, Christians and Muslims, are killing each other, all in the name of God or religion.

Robert Wuthnow in *American Mythos* maintains that Americans think that they are religious, but they shy away from making too public a display of religion, or their cry is, "I do not need a church." He also states that even though Americans have become tolerant of diversity, we still have difficulty working for the common good because of rampant individualism. How much of this applies to Christians?

The Challenge of Jesus

Jesus challenges us to love our enemies (Luke 6:27). This requires a deeper commitment because our love will be met with hatred, our good works with bad ones. If we have a difficult time getting along with a family member or our next-door neighbor, how can we possibly love our enemies? Is our Christianity a pretense where we ignore the elephant in the room? A seminarian once asked a bishop, "How can we love our enemies when most of the time we don't even respond to love with love?" He replied, "My son, if you cannot love your enemy, hate him a little less each day." We can disagree with someone and still offer the individual a handshake of peace. We fear relationships or getting to know others better because it might change both of us. Tolerance will always fall short of loving "with all one's mind, heart, and soul."

Jesus never used the word *tolerance* but often acted in apparently opposite ways. He accepted prostitutes and tax collectors, and he cured lepers. When the Canaanite woman (a Gentile who belonged to the old Canaanite stock who hated the Jews) approached him, the apostles asked Jesus to get rid of her, but he said, "I was sent only to the lost sheep of the house of Israel" (Matt 15:21–28). The woman pleaded with him not for herself but for her daughter. He said to her, "It is not fair to take the children's food and throw it to the dogs." Her humble response was, "Yes, Lord, yet even the dogs eat the crumbs that fall from their master's table" (Matt 15:24–27). That made Jesus aware of her great faith, which broadened his vision of culture and traditions and changed his attitude.

The apostles wanted to call down destruction on a Samaritan town that did not accept Jesus. He said no. To Peter, who had a difficult time accepting Jesus' suffering and death, he said, "Get behind me, Satan! You are a stumbling block to me; for you are setting your mind not on divine things but on human things" (Matt 16:23). Despite the apostles' misunderstanding, Jesus continued to love them for their inability to receive his message and mission.

Jesus invited Zacchaeus to come down from his sycamore tree and dine with him. To dine with someone at that time meant there was a close, intimate relationship. No wonder the people grumbled, saying "He has gone to be the guest of one who is a sinner" (Luke 19:7). This encounter deeply affected Zacchaeus, who was willing to pay back fourfold those he had cheated. Later, Jesus more than tolerated the Samaritan woman at the well who didn't want anything to do with him. "How is it that you, a Jew, ask a drink of me, a woman of Samaria?" (John 4:9). Yet she ends up becoming a disciple bringing the good news to others.

He also dined with Simon the Pharisee, and Jesus pointed out to Simon his lack of good manners. He cured the son of a Roman centurion who did not consider himself worthy to have him come under his roof. Jesus was tolerant of the woman caught in adultery. He saw the good in others, not the bad. He was willing to tolerate the flaws in people's lives because he saw how their inner goodness reflected that they were children of God. His tolerance reached its climax on the cross when he forgave the good thief and forgave those who nailed him to the cross by saying, "Father, forgive them; for they do not know what they are doing" (Luke 23:34). That message will always be a challenge for us when we are deeply hurt and we find it hard to forgive. Forgiveness, as will be considered later, is a crucial test of how Christian we are.

Most of us are hurting, but the question remains, where are we hurting? Is it from rejection, humiliation, disappointment, or some indignity, which results in bitterness, coldness, cynicism, or anger? We often say we are fine when actually our hearts are bleeding, our fists are clenched. At these times, we need to enter our own brokenness, restlessness, and inadequacies by having recourse to prayer. Prayer will bring us the peace we need and the ability to surrender to a loving, understanding God.

Jesus' tolerance, however, had limits, as is evident when he went into the temple area and found the moneychangers there. He was intolerant of systemic injustice where the moneychangers were overcharging people. He overturned their tables and cried out, "Take these things out of here! Stop making my Father's house a marketplace!" (John 2:16). He drove these moneychangers out of the temple but not out of the country. He also made some of his most scathing remarks against the scribes and Pharisees, calling them hypocrites because they burdened others with laws and regulations and forgot the most important law of love. They had more than six hundred rules and regulations, many pertaining to the Sabbath observance. For example, if you sprained your wrist on the Sabbath, one was not allowed to attend to it. Thank God, however, women were allowed to give birth on the Sabbath!

Tolerance Elusive

Theodore Roosevelt, as well as Woodrow Wilson, encouraged Americans not to look upon themselves as Italian, Irish, German, or Jewish Americans, but as Americans. These presidents did not want a 50–50 or a hyphenated allegiance, but a total commitment as Americans. They envisioned a "melting pot" based on a play by that title written by Israel Zangwell, where all the rivalries and hatreds were set aside and a new nation would emerge. The only problem was, according to Michael Novak, a philosopher and historian, there were Americans who were "unmeltable ethnics," like the Native Americans who endured broken treaties and unjust resettlement.

It is difficult for us to reconcile that the First Article of the United States Constitution states that "Indians were not to be counted," and African Americans were "three-fifths of a person." Where did the other two-fifth's disappear? For 240 years, African Americans living here in the United States were tolerated as slaves. Now they make up 13 percent of the population, but 39 percent of the prison population, according to the U.S. Department of Justice—nearly a million African Americans in all.

As Christians, we need to abandon the image of a melting pot where attempts are made to force people to be what they are not. Jesus never forced individuals to be what they were not but invited them to follow him. Soon people of Anglo-Saxon ancestry will not be in the majority in the United States, so we need to focus on greater tolerance of other groups rather than becoming a melting pot. Maybe we need to reread and pray over the Pentecost event where Parthians, Medes, Elamites, Asians, Phrygians, and Romans heard the same message in their own native language (Acts 2:6–11). God spoke to them as they were, not as what God wanted them to become.

A possible image of our nation, as well as others, could be a salad bowl or a stew. Each item is different but also enriches the final product. The radishes don't say to the croutons, "I don't need you." The meat does not say to the carrots, "I don't need you." They all blend together to add flavor and zest to the finished product. The group that gathered on that first Pentecost acts as a model and reminder of what we strive to become. We need a new Pentecost where God will show us how to tolerate the differences between the various groups.

In 2002, Gallup conducted a poll of both the "churched" and the "unchurched." The only significant difference between the two groups was that one frequented church and the other did not. There was no difference in the areas of infidelity in marriage, lying, cheating on income tax, and stealing. What Gallup termed the "highly spiritual" Christians (only 12 percent!) manifested that they were happier, more satisfied with life, were tolerant of other races and religions, and were interested in helping society to become better.[1] Where would we fit in?

Intolerance

We need to tear down the walls and fences of intolerance. That is our challenge. Robert Frost wrote that there is something about intolerance that does not love or build up a wall. That poetry verse might be changed to read that Christians should not become or build up a wall. A wall certainly existed between Germany and its Jewish community. Yet, finally, a few years ago, to mark the fifty-eighth anniversary of the Auschwitz death camp's liberation, an accord was signed putting the Jewish community on a legal par with main Christian churches. The hope is that this historic signing will alleviate anti-Semitism and racism in Germany.

Silence and ignorance often breed intolerance. Some of the silent forms of intolerance are the shrugging of shoulders, the rolling of the eyes, the turning of one's back, the raising of eyebrows. We need to drain the swamp of intolerance that leads to fear, frustration, and futility. Our society might be characterized in fishing terms: "You fish on your side, I'll fish on my side, and nobody fishes in the middle."

Rosa Parks, a black woman from Montgomery, Alabama, refused to give up her seat in a bus although she knew that she might risk injury or even death. She did not lose her life, only her livelihood, because no one would hire her after that incident. However, she realized how unjust, unfair, and oppressive it was to give up her seat. Enough was enough! She set in motion a boycott of buses that lasted for almost a year.

Oppression will continue, however, as long as the oppressed tolerate it. The same can be said of abused spouses or children. Rosa Parks has left us a legacy of courage to counteract any abusive unfairness. We still continue racial profiling or saying things about others as long as we don't say them too loudly. The conflicts between Palestinians and Israeli, Irish Catholics and Protestants, gay and straight, Muslim and Christians, continues to boil. So many of our issues are put into a win/lose paradigm.

The war with Iraq and the acceptance of homosexuality are both examples of the issues viewed in the context of a win/lose paradigm. This paradigm also prevents us from respecting the beliefs of Hindus, Muslims, Jews, and other religions. As Keith Russell, the editor of *The Living Pulpit,* has stated, "In evangelical Christian theology the cross is not a weapon but a symbol of God's love and compassion for all creation. We do not need to go to war! The battle has already been fought and won. We, the church, simply need to live our lives and make our witness in the light of this already achieved eschatological reality of God's redemptive acts."[2] This is challenging indeed.

The story is told about Bishop Desmond Tutu, who was walking down the sidewalk in South Africa. He was met by a white man walking the other way who snarled at him, "Move off the sidewalk! I don't give way to gorillas." The Bishop calmly replied as he gestured him to pass, "Ah, yes, but I do." What a marvelous and humorous way to turn the other cheek. It undoubtedly unnerved the racist man who had made the remark.

We are at a crossroads where we must choose greater destruction and evil, or greater compassion, love, understanding, and peace toward people of another race, religion, or ethnicity. Once the stranger has become our neighbor, love of God and ourselves makes more sense. Yet, the struggle of good and evil continues. As Saint Thomas Aquinas maintains, evil is nothing, just the absence of good. Evil can be compared to a giant spider web. Touch it anywhere and you set the whole web in motion. Our sins have an effect on others, especially social sins such as racism and sexism.

What we need to remember is that God is not the cause of evil. God might permit it, as was true with Job. God accompanies us in our pain. I remember in Louisiana, I came across a mother who gave birth to two blind children. Her third pregnancy also resulted in another blind child. The father could not take this cross, so he left her. Certainly God brought strength to this mother as God did to Joshua, who was told not to be afraid when he was about to lead the Israelites over the Jordan River. God told Isaiah that he could walk through fire and not get burned. Jesus assured his apostles when their boat was being tossed by the waves, "Take heart, it is I; do not be afraid" (Matt 14:27). As the poet Theodore Roethke wrote, when experiencing a dark time the eye begins to see; this demands much faith and trust in a loving God.

We need to look at the cross and remember that God allowed this to happen to his precious Son. Some years ago, I heard of a teenager who was in a serious car accident. He was taken to a nearby hospital and declared dead on arrival. When the mother arrived, she screamed at the priest saying, "Where was God when my son died?" He calmly responded, "The same place God was when his Son died on the cross." Life truly is a mystery to be lived and not solved. Think of all the psychic energy we expend trying to solve it. As Christians we are invited to enter into the mystery and live it as fully as we can.

President George W. Bush's now famous (or infamous) phrase "the axis of evil" has been quoted often. He believed that nations opposed to ours need to be confronted or eliminated to safeguard our freedom. But isn't freedom more than a materialistic and consumer lifestyle? Fake lines have been drawn in the sand between the good guys and the villains, so that saber rattlers will see war as inevitable. Isn't our present war in Iraq really just a solution for the ailing economy? Is this the point of view that we, as Christians, should hold?

Christians need to protest against all animosities and divisions. Hatred and discrimination must not be tolerated. Millions of Americans are born into poverty; women are not receiving equal rights; one out of six children grows up hungry in the wealthiest country on earth; capital punishment is rarely used upon the rich; abortions are performed everyday; euthanasia is becoming a viable option for treating the terminally ill; the greed of CEOs puts thousands of people out of work; snide remarks are made about lesbians, gays, African Americans, and Latinos. Immigrants are often looked upon as a burden upon our economy. Many are considered terrorists, and some are kept in detention centers unjustly. How do we prevent illigal immigrants from entering the United States?

Bill Richardson, governor of New Mexico, declared that we could build a 700-mile fence seventy feet high to keep the illegal immigrants out, but they would get a ladder over seventy feet high to climb over the fence. Do we allow these individuals to stay a certain amount of time before sending them home? Do we increase penalties on employers who hire them? Doesn't the inscription on the Statue of Liberty proclaim, "Give me your tired, your poor, your huddled masses yearning to breathe free"? What would Jesus say about the plight of thirteen million refugees, half of whose children will never see a doctor? Or about a country that is robbing the poor to feed the military? The United States is spending more on war and armaments than all the countries in the world combined. Congress has reduced forty billion dollars of funding to Medicare and Medicaid, thus endangering the health and welfare of many.

Whole cities in the Third World could live on the garbage we throw away. The average American throws away one hundred pounds of usable food every year. Our criminal justice system often violates basic rights because it is not impartial, fair, or just to the poor and jobless. We have as a nation sneered at the Kyoto accords, the World Court, and arms control treaties. None of us is completely innocent or without blame.

In physics, metal has a tolerance or breaking point. Too much stress and the metal will break. The same is true in a relationship: too much stress can fracture it or a community. How much stress it takes to reach the breaking point is difficult to measure. How do we react when a woman is battered by a spouse or when a community suffers from racism? At times one act of intolerance can be a time bomb setting off riots and other serious consequences.

Keith Russell pointedly asks, "How do we build a new human community amidst the differences of religion, race, gender, and culture? How do we address the proclivity toward violence that emerges in the church and among religious people? Is violence our only recourse? Ignorance and arrogance seem to be the bedrock of intolerance."[3]

Christians can take a prophetic stance in decrying these injustices. People like Dorothy Day, Cesar Chavez, Thomas Merton,

Thea Bowman, Sister Helen Prejean, and others have certainly shaped us in our thinking and acting. They were not afraid to speak the truth in love, inviting us to go beyond tolerance, opening our minds and hearts to the poor, migrant workers, street people, African Americans, and those who have taken a strong stand against war. Former Secretary of Defense Donald Rumsfeld said things that made excellent sound bytes but amounted to questionable diplomacy. Iraq has been compared to Pandora's box, and we are now experiencing the demons that have been freed since the lid was removed.

Bishop Gumbleton of Detroit was deeply influenced by his own gay brother. In 1997, he initiated and coauthored a pastoral letter of the United States Bishops that was entitled *Always Our Children*. He now has become a "prophet of tolerance" for the lesbian and gay community. He sees a dichotomy because they "are encouraged to accept and love themselves as they are...but on the other hand they must keep secret the fact they are homosexual when engaged in their ministry." He maintains, "I believe our community would be enriched by the acknowledged presence of homosexual teachers in our schools."[4] He advocates creating a climate where young people are able to hear the voices of gays and lesbians, and he believes they can learn how to be more tolerant and loving from this exposure.

I attended a lecture given by Bishop Gumbleton in Milwaukee, Wisconsin. He described how he reacted wrongly when he found out that his brother was a homosexual. Later, after much prayer and meditation, his conversion helped him to respond to his mother's question, "Is my son going to hell? He assured her that he certainly was not.

Jesus made it clear that he did not tolerate any harm done to "little ones." Our Catholic bishops have endorsed a controversial zero-tolerance stand against anyone who sexually abuses children. Such behavior ought to be abhorred and addressed. Betrayals and violations of the sexually abused can only be fully understood by the victims themselves or by their therapists. Often an inner rage is present, ready to explode. These violations must never be condoned, but those who have done them must be forgiven as Jesus forgave. As Christians we need to offer solace, help, and consolation to victims and their families, asking for their forgiveness in the name of the church because we are the church. We also need to address society's struggle with pedophiles returning to our communities. No community wants these individuals living in its neighborhood, and they have been compared to modern-day lepers.

So our challenge as Christians is to be tolerant when necessary, as well as intolerant. A delicate balance exists between accepting others and rejecting social injustices. Both, as we have seen, have their limitations, and we need to move beyond them to loftier realities in our pluralistic society. When will back fences become places of conversation rather than signs of division? Another analogy might be to leave our tolerances on the shore, meet in the middle of the lake, and catch enough fish to feed others. Like Jesus we need to emphasize compassion and forgiveness. God is accessible to people of all religions. Love is much broader than tolerance, and, as Saint Paul assures us, love will never fail. We need to comfort the afflicted and afflict the comfortable, which is exactly what Jesus did.

⁂ ⁂ ⁂

SCRIPTURE PASSAGES FOR REFLECTION

"Woman, great is your faith! Let it be done for you as you wish."
(Matt 15:28)

"He has gone to be the guest of one who is a sinner." (Luke 19:7)

"How is it that you, a Jew, ask a drink of me, a woman of Samaria?"
(John 4:9)

*"Take these things out of here! Stop making my Father's house a
marketplace!* (John 2:16)

QUESTIONS TO CONSIDER

1. As Christians, how do we move beyond tolerance?

2. How can we fight the forms of hatred in our society?

3. How do we stretch our understanding of religious
   traditions?

4. How do we build up walls of intolerance?

5. How do we protest against animosities and divisions
   like racism and sexism?

5

THE DARK SIDE OF ENMITY

"You have heard that it was said, 'An eye for an eye, and a tooth for a tooth.' But I say to you, do not resist an evildoer."
Matt 5:38–39

Even if we find a balance between tolerance and intolerance, as Christians we still have to contend with enmity in our own lives and certainly in the world. Why would Christians even want to consider this topic?

The world itself is rather gruesome and harsh. A cursory glance at our world today convinces us how important it is to address this subject because of all the violence and hatred that is present. Various groups manifest this continuous violence: Palestinians and Israelis, Hutus and Tutsis, Hindus and Muslims, Christians and Muslims, Catholics and Protestants in Ireland, just to name a few. The attacks on World Trade Center and the Pentagon building still remain etched in our memories. Enmity is boundless, indifferent to race, gender, class, or age.

The Greek word for enmity is *echtho,* which means to hate or despise someone. Enmity can arise from rivalry, distorted notions of who is right, competition, greed, not accepting one's limitations, or alienation from God and others. The results are that people become victimized, dehumanized, dominated, and alienated. We can understand how the wall of enmity is built, brick by brick, maybe not as stately as the walls of Jericho or China, but it is built with bricks of hostility, fear, revenge, unforgivingness, resentment, and anger.

The wall can also act as protection from additional pain, so we continue lashing out at others. We legitimized our stand on the Iraq war as a preemptive strike because of the terrorist attacks of September 11. President Bush dubbed some nations the "axis of evil," creating a doctrine of retaliation. The spiritual toxicity runs deep. The venom and bile caused by enmity diminishes our needed energy to love others as Jesus loved.

Pope John Paul II insisted that the September 11 attacks must not lead to a deepening of divisions, and religion cannot be used as a reason for the conflict. Pope Benedict XVI is a strong critic of war because it results in much hatred and bloodshed. The theme for his message on World Day of Peace 2007, was *The Human Person, the Heart of Peace,* in which he emphasized the respect needed for the human person that will bring peace.

Biblical Aspect

The biblical aspect of enmity can be traced back to the story of Adam and Eve when God said, "I will put enmity between you and the woman, and between your offspring and hers" (Gen 3:15). The amazing part is that God is responsible, but the enmity enters the world because of the disobedience of Adam and Eve. The cunning serpent tempted Eve by telling her she could eat of the tree in the middle of the garden. The serpent assured her that she would not die, but that her eyes would be opened and "you will be like God, knowing good and evil" (Gen 3:4–5). Being like God is still the basic sin. Whenever the relationship of Creator and creature is disrupted, there is sin that often arises because of enmity.

In Numbers, we read "in enmity strikes another with the hand, and death ensues, then the one who struck the blow shall be put to death" (Num 35:21). Premeditated murder is envisioned in this passage where an individual plans how to kill another person. Here the enmity is between human beings, and not a serpent and a human person. The Cain and Abel story also is a graphic description of enmity. The enmity is spreading like a cancer.

In Ezekiel we read, "Thus says the Lord God: Because of unending hostilities the Philistines acted in vengeance, and with malice of the heart took revenge in destruction; therefore, thus says the Lord God, I will stretch out my hand against the Philistines, cut off the Cherethites, and destroy the rest of the seacoast" (Ezek 25:15–16). God is accusing the Philistines of acting vengefully toward Judah as well as God. Here the enmity spreads beyond relationships to whole nations, and the enmity is *undying*. That is one of the key words.

Ezekiel also accuses the nation of Edom of enmity when he proclaimed, "Because you cherished an ancient enmity, and gave over the people of Israel to the power of the sword at the time of their calamity, at the time of their final punishment; therefore, as I live, says the Lord God, I will prepare you for blood, and blood shall pursue you; since you did not hate bloodshed, bloodshed shall pursue you" (Ezek 35:5–6). The Lord will also make Edom an eternal desolation, a wasteland without any inhabitants. Enmity begets enmity, just as violence begets violence.

In the Second Book of Kings, we read about the king of Aram who ordered his soldiers to take the prophet Elisha captive because he was helping the king of Israel. When Elisha saw the huge force of horses, chariots, and soldiers, he prayed to the Lord, "Strike this people, please, with blindness" and they were struck blind. He then led them to Samaria where he prayed that their eyes would be opened, and so they were. The king of Israel wanted to kill them, but Elisha said no, "Set food and water before them so that they may eat and drink, and let them go to their master. So he prepared for them a great feast; after they ate and drank, he sent them on their way, and they went to their master. And the Arameans no longer came raiding into the land of Israel" (2 Kings 6:18–23). The logical approach for the king of Israel was to kill his adversaries. Elisha, however, reminds the king that these soldiers are not his prisoners and therefore he cannot kill them. Asking the king to feed them instead was indeed revolutionary. But that strategy breaks the enmity and vicious cycle of violence.

As Christians we can ask why Jesus shared bread with Judas even though he knew that he was about to betray him. Maybe Saint Paul was aware of the Elisha story when he wrote, "If your enemies are hungry, feed them; if they are thirsty, give them something to drink; for by doing this you will heap burning coals upon their heads. Do not be overcome by evil, but overcome evil with good" (Rom 12:20). But is our faith strong enough that when people hate or despise us we don't retaliate? Is our faith strong enough to trust God rather than the Dow Jones numbers or our savings account?

As was evident in the Hebrew Scriptures, national and personal enemies always existed, and they lashed out against the prophets. Syria and Israel were perennial enemies. Enmity was also present in the Israelite community. Personal enemies were personified in Esau and Jacob, Moses and Pharaoh, David and Goliath, Saul and David, David and Absalom. These are fascinating stories that have been retold many times, especially the David and Goliath story. Goliath shows nothing but contempt for David saying, "Am I a dog, that you come to me with sticks?" (1 Sam 17:43). We know the rest of the story.

We notice enmity also in the New Testament with Herod, who wanted to kill Jesus, and Herodias, who asked for the head of John the Baptist. The scribes and Pharisees were constantly plotting how to do away with Jesus. Saul nurtured tremendous animosity toward Christians before his conversion. Saint Paul experienced many problems, especially with the church in Corinth, and underwent many sufferings, particularly from false brothers (cf. 2 Cor 11:23–29). Even today an insatiable desire exists for these kind of stories as is evident from the popularity of westerns, spy novels, and movies such as *Jaws* and *Lord of the Rings*. Saint James warned the people of his time, "Do you not know that friendship with the world is enmity with God?" (Jas 4:4)

We don't find, however, the word enmity as plentiful in the New Testament. We find a different kind of struggle arises from another kind of enemy. Saint Paul states, "For our struggle is not against enemies of blood and flesh, but against the rulers, against the authorities, against the cosmic powers of this present darkness, against the spiritual forces of evil in the heavenly places" (Eph 6:12). This enemy is rather impersonal, not having flesh and blood; it is widespread and has no boundaries; it is as automatic as flipping on a light switch.

A good example of this kind of struggle is Jesus' encounter with the demons from two Gadarene demoniacs (Matt 8:28–34). They asked to be sent into the swine to save themselves, but ended up being destroyed. Today's fascination with the unseen is brought out in movies involving sharks. Sharks are good examples of this type of enemy. They are impersonal because they can't be seen on the surface. They are widespread because they often swim in schools. They are killers because they will eat anything. No wonder the movie *Jaws* had such an impact on people.

Maybe our real enemies today are the kinds that include many *isms*. As Christians we have to be aware of the more clever ones like corporations that lie to their employees, employers who export jobs to other countries where workers receive less pay. We might include some politicians who employ questionable advertising tactics against their opponents to get elected. What about church and state leaders who have feet of clay? What about hospitals and nursing homes that cut their staffs, resulting in patients who are not properly attended? The list could be extended to include all those who act impersonally and automatically treat others like a number. Much ink has been spilled on all the animosity these events have caused. Much faith is needed to counteract these situations so that our faith will never crash like a computer or need to be programmed.

Another form of enmity might be scapegoating. According to Rene Girard, an historian and philosophical anthropologist, scapegoating destroys joy. We are often held together by having someone to hate, someone to be against. What binds us together is a common enemy. Girard believes there are no exceptions because historical alliances prove his point. We have to admit that it is much easier to blame someone else than to accept responsibilities for ourselves. It's the pope's fault, the bishop's fault, the pastor's fault, the boss's fault. Recall how much flack God received as a result of the tsunami, or all the blame heaped on others because of Hurricane Katrina.

The origin of scapegoating can be traced back to the sixteenth chapter of Leviticus. A priest would lay his hands on a goat, confessing the sins of the Israelite people, and then send the goat out into the desert. Girard believes this is one of the most ingenious rites ever invented. The Dead Sea scrolls reveal that the goat's head was laden with thorns, a purple cloak put on it, and then spat upon. Certainly, this reminds us of Jesus and his passion. Do we honor or worship one of the greatest scapegoats?

Girard believes that when we are in pain we usually will pass it on to someone else. Now we can pass our pain on to Jesus so we don't have to burden another. Jesus takes on our inclination to scapegoat. Jesus accepts hatred but does not return it. How easy it is for us to crucify someone else's good name, but Jesus refuses to do this. How easy it is for us to seek vengeance, but Jesus does not. Girard maintains that the only way to counteract scapegoating is through a spiritual transformation. We need to stop playing this game and become adult Christians by not blaming, accusing, attacking, shaming, and hating others. When we are blamed, falsely accused, attacked, shamed, or hated, we sometimes have to respond with nonresistance.

Jesus and Nonresistance

Jesus offers a challenge of nonresistance but not acquiescence. Injustices should never be accepted as just. Jesus said, "You have heard that it was said, 'An eye for an eye, and a tooth for a tooth.' But I say to you, do not resist an evildoer. But if anyone strikes you on the right cheek, turn the other also; and if anyone wants to sue you and take your coat, give your cloak as well; and if anyone forces you to go one mile, go also the second mile. Give to everyone who begs from you, and do not refuse anyone who wants to borrow from you" (Matt 5:38–42).

One day I was explaining this passage to a group of grade-school children, and I asked one of them what he would do if someone slapped him on his cheek. He responded without hesitation, "I would run." The only way someone can slap us on our right cheek is with the back of his hand. That was a worse insult to a Jew. Turning the other cheek certainly does not mean we have to become a doormat. What it means is we become a lightning rod to ward off hostile attackers. It means not to retaliate or get even.

Acts of turning the other cheek, offering one's cloak, going the extra mile, and offering hard-earned money are excessive in emphasizing the injustice, but that is what authentic Christians are encouraged to do. As Bruce Chilton, a professor of religion at Bard College in New York, explains, "Instead of an eye for an eye, it suggests a cheek after a cheek. This is nonresistance; it is exemplary response. That is, it is a form of retaliation: not to harm but to show another way."[1]

We have to show how this command of Jesus applies to communities or nations as well. Many continue to question our pre-emptive strike against Iraq. Most people believe that war is a tragedy. It often makes international relationships worse rather than better. We have to find ways to discuss important issues without resorting to angry animosities, resentful feelings, or harsh and hostile words. We need to learn to live with our enemies rather than try to eradicate them through war or "winning at all costs." When inflicting violence on others, we will have to pay the last penny as Jesus said (Matt 5:26). Or will God inflict punishment on "children for the iniquity of parents, to the third and fourth generation" (Exod 20:5)? We use our flags as symbols of what we stand for as nations, but we also use them to shroud our caskets. Video games and television show us how to settle disputes by engaging in violence. Whom do we fight once the enemies vanish?

We often aren't responsible for enmity directed against us, but we are responsible for how we react. We are often reactors rather than reflectors. The need to respond with nonviolence is indeed challenging. Dorothy Day has been characterized as a "Mother Teresa with a past." She became a "seamless garment" championing the cause of nonviolence. Others like Dr. Martin Luther King Jr., Gandhi, Bishop Desmond Tutu, and especially Jesus show us the way. When we retaliate, we are no better than those who inflict harm on us, just a little less messy.

Jesus' Message of Love

Jesus also said, "Love your enemies, do good to those who hate you, bless those who curse you, pray for those who abuse you" (Luke 6:27–28). This again is a reversal similar to many other gospel messages that Jesus spoke about: "The last shall be first." "Those who want to save their life will lose it." "The Son of Man came not to be served but to serve." However, of all the instructions that Jesus gave his apostles, to love one's enemies was the most challenging. At this command, our Christian spirituality and social justice definitely intersect. The implication is that those who hate, curse, and mistreat us are the enemy.

Jonathan Swift, the English satirist, wrote that we have just enough religion to make us hate and oppress others, but not enough to make us love one another. The Israelite people were under the impression they could worship God, and, at the same time, oppress others. Amos gives God's answer: "The offerings of well-being of your fatted animals I will not look upon…But let justice roll down like waters, and righteousness like an ever-flowing stream" (Amos 5:21–24).

The Good Samaritan story contrasts the Jews and Samaritans, who were considered the outsiders and not capable of doing much good. That is why this parable of Jesus shocked his listeners. Samaritans were the enemy, but in this story one Samaritan does what was least expected, being a good neighbor and showing compassion and mercy to someone in pain. The story also removes biases, prejudices, and other negative concepts towards the Samaritan. The parable can and ought to be used by Christians as an antidote to enmity, especially its spiritual and social implications.

The story is told of a couple married for forty-nine years who were facing a most critical time in their lives. The wife had contracted cancer and needed to undergo surgery. During the operation, the husband paced back and forth in the waiting room. Finally, the Japanese doctor emerged and told the husband that the operation was a success. The greatly relieved husband, who had fought against the Japanese during World War II, gave the doctor a huge embrace. Previously, he always had maintained much hostility against the Japanese. However, this moment became a healing and turning point in his life. What will enable us to have a similar transformation?

Prayer

Saint Paul prayed, "For if while we were enemies, we were reconciled to God through the death of his Son, much more surely, having been reconciled, will we be saved by his life" (Rom 5:10). Maybe the first enemy is not our persecutors but ourselves because of our sinful relationship to God and others. In the Our Father, we pray as Jesus taught us, "forgive us our debts, as we also have forgiven our debtors" (Matt 6:12). Jesus prayed on the cross, "Father, forgive them; for they do not know what they are doing" (Luke 23:34). Stephen, the first Christian martyr cried out, "Lord, do not hold this sin against them" (Acts 7:60).

Prayer helps to alleviate the pain of the oppressor and leads to transformation in our lives. Prayer enables people to deal more effectively with conflict, violence, and other social evils. Praying in this way implies a risk, the risk of being changed or transformed. How many of us are willing to give up our prejudices or biases, or risk being transformed? A radical transformation is possible because with God all things are possible.

Christians claim that they live up to moral standards and the belief that God can change their lives. However, surveys do not substantiate these claims because racism, sexism, immoral sexual behavior, money, greed, consumerism, and materialism have made inroads into their lives. Christians need to have their toes stepped on and their consciences seared even if it might cause pain and make them wince. It is difficult to face hard, obvious facts about ourselves, to be diagnosed as not healthy and in need of strong medicine. However, if the prescription is followed, it will change our lives.

Tim Flannery, an internationally acclaimed scientist, has shown the impact of climate change on our planet. We might ask has there been a Christian "climate change" in our spiritual lives? He maintains that one of the best sources of information about climate is a piece of timber. He writes: "Look at a piece of timber, and you can see, written in its fine texture and growth rings, a story of the way things were when the tree lived. Widely space rings tell of warm and bountiful growing seasons, when the sun shone and rain fell at the right time. Compressed rings, recording little growth in the tree, tell of adversity when long, hard winters or drought-blighted summers tested life to the limits."[2] What if we could examine our spiritual lives in the same way?

The Israelites were sent into exile because of their turning away from God and community. Are we not witnessing today a turning away from God by Christians who are accepting the practices of abortions, sexual immorality, and the esteeming of money, greed, and selfishness in society? Does history repeat itself? Will the call of repentance by our modern-day prophets go unheeded as it did with the Israelites?

Rebecca Radillo, Professor of Pastoral Care New York Theological Seminary quotes Walter Wink, a Biblical professor: "If God is compassionate toward us with all our unredeemed evil, then God must treat our enemies the same way. As we begin to acknowledge our own inner shadow, we become more tolerant of the shadow of others. As we begin to love the enemy within, we develop the compassion we need to love the enemy without."[3] Rage and revenge must be converted into concern and compassion for the offender.

Saint Paul states how Jesus reconciles us with God, "in one body through the cross, thus putting to death that hostility through it" (Eph 2:16). It is the cross that teaches us what to do with our enmity or hostility. As Christians we have to avoid the extremes of downplaying the cross and suffering as well as joy and the resurrection. We need to balance them by fully accepting both. Jesus showed us how to do this. Through prayer we let go of our pride and become more humble; we become more aware of how we have wounded others; we learn what true forgiveness really means, and then proclaim his death until he comes again. We need to ask ourselves who we are, the people on the cross or the crowd doing the nailing. As someone has said, we need to look good on wood.

Enmity in the Church

Enmity within the church or parish is especially evident now. The level of conflict has certainly increased with the strong desire to get even or to "overthrow" those in authority. For many it has become a power struggle. Some pastors experience this at their meetings. Some parishioners have a penchant to "chip away" or ankle bite their pastors. Is this part of a culture that is bent on retaliation or on win/lose situations?

Keith Russell, editor of *The Living Pulpit,* maintains, "In some ways the church is simply playing out the larger drama that is happening in Iraq, Palestine, and Afghanistan. We have been affected by our culture in a primary way and are, both implicitly and explicitly, giving justification to the American culture of vengeance and retaliation. The church's fights give, in kind of a backhanded way, religious justification for the war on terror."[4]

Saint Paul quotes scripture when he wrote, "Vengeance is mine, I will repay, says the Lord" (Rom 12:19). So vengeance is not our job; nonviolence is. Why are we so quick to follow the spirit of retaliation, especially after September 11? We rationalized our approach because of what was done to us. What road are we following: the broad road that leads to destruction or the narrow road that leads to peace and justice? We need to look within our own parishes, communities, and lives to alleviate any animosity there before even addressing the larger problems. So the "worship wars" go on in parishes. People complain about the music, the songs that are sung, the length of the service, whether we kneel or stand, and the preaching, just to name a few.

The casualties are anger, resentment, hurt, and alienation. We become tone deaf in our discussions. Some worship committees resemble the Nuclear Regulatory Commission in their posturing. The saying is still true that we reap what we sow. Many who need to change their harvest have to refrain from hurting others, seeking revenge, carrying grudges. If we are causing others to suffer, we are also transmitting violence. It is much easier to say, "I can't do anything about violence." Actually, we can. Our own hatred, fear, revenge, and resentment can in some instances cause more damage than any terrorist.

Ali Bardakoglu, head of the state-run religious affairs directorate in Turkey, accused Pope Benedict XVI of being "full of enmity and grudge" because of his remarks about Islam.[5]

Nothing could be further from the truth, but Pope Benedict XVI did apologize.

Richard Rohr, OFM, puts it well, "Catholics have no ability to carry the dark side of the church either, nor the dark side of the papacy, nor the dark side of the clergy. It is always all good or all bad, never 'both crucified and resurrected at the same time,' as Jesus is...We refuse to carry the dark side of institutions, of groups, nations, of periods of history. We look for races and nations to blame, instead of admitting that we are in this human thing together. Every culture, in my opinion, is a mixture of darkness and light."[6] We want everything black or white, or everything spelled out for us in the smallest detail. Gray areas exist and we have to take more responsibility for our own actions if we are to be truly free.

Today we need Christians to proclaim boldly reconciliation, nonviolence, love, forgiveness, and peace. By living with enmity in our hearts, we become our worst enemies. We alienate ourselves from others and especially from God. We are challenged to see with fresh eyes. We also need to listen more intently so we can remove our walls of distrust brick by brick if necessary. We must rely more on God than our own walls of hate. We need to tear down any walls that we might have built against our enemies.

President Lincoln said that he would destroy his enemies by making them friends. He tried to carry that out in his life and had to suffer just as Jesus suffered carrying out his message of nonresistance and love. We are asked to do the same.

⚜ ⚜ ⚜

SCRIPTURE PASSAGES FOR REFLECTION

"I will put enmity between you and the woman, and between your offspring and hers." (Gen 3:15)

"Set food and water before them so that they may eat and drink." (2 Kgs 6:22)

"If anyone strikes you on the right cheek, turn the other also." (Matt 5:39)

"Do not be overcome by evil, but overcome evil with good." (Rom 12:21)

"Do you not know that friendship with the world is enmity with God." (Jas 4:4)

QUESTIONS TO CONSIDER

1. Do we build up a wall to protect us from hurts?

2. What are some of more clever forms of enmity we contend with?

3. Do we *scapegoat* and in what situations?

4. How can we turn the other cheek?

5. How can we discuss important issues without resorting to animosity or harsh words?

6. Is enmity present in our parish community? If so, how do we counteract it?

6

DARE WE *CARE-FRONT*?

*"If another member of the church sins against you, go and
point out the fault when the two of you are alone."*
Matt 18:15

Christians who do not reach out to others, are intolerant of others, or harbor violence and enmity certainly need to be confronted. One of the gospel counsels that few Christians carry out in their lives is in the area of confrontation. Often we find ourselves in a position where we need to confront someone and we feel powerless to do this. Even the word *confront* sounds ominous and fearful. I prefer using the word *care-front* rather than *confront* for reasons that will be pointed out.[1]

Care-front means that we really care for the individual and desire that person's growth. God is pictured in the scriptures as a caring God, a God of consolation, but also a disturbing God. When God asked Adam and Eve, "Where are you?" God asked a very important and caring question. It is the same question that God asks us: "Where are you in your relationship to me, to others, and to yourself?" When God asked Cain where Abel was, that was a caring question. God asks us also whether we value others enough to be concerned about them.

The prophets continued to show this care for God's people. Isaiah said: "Do not fear for I am with you, do not be afraid, for

I am your God; I will strengthen you, I will help you, I will uphold you with my victorious right hand" (Isa 41:10). He could also speak of the Lord in this fashion: "His lips are full of indignation, and his tongue is like a devouring fire" (Isa 30:27). Jeremiah could say of God: "I have loved you with an everlasting love; therefore I have continued my faithfulness to you" (Jer 31:3). But he also said: "Cursed are those who trust in mere mortals and make mere flesh their strength, whose hearts turn away from the Lord" (Jer 17:5). Ezekiel expressed God's care in this fashion: "I will seek the lost, and I will bring back the strayed, and I will bind up the injured, and I will strengthen the weak, but the fat and strong I will destroy. I will feed them with justice" (Ezek 34:16). These and other prophets showed how God was not only a consoling God but a disturbing God.

But all these prophets pale into insignificance with the coming of Jesus. John the Baptist announced his coming and was not afraid to *care-front* by stating: "Repent, for the kingdom of heaven has come near" (Matt 3:2). When he saw the Pharisees and Sadducees he said, "You brood of vipers! Who warned you to flee from the wrath to come. Bear fruit worthy of repentance" (Matt 3:7–8). He was not afraid to *care-front* Herod who had married Herodias, the wife of his brother Philip, and even suffered the consequences by being beheaded (Mark 6:17–18).

No one *care-fronted*, however, the way Jesus did. He was not only willing to console people by his many miracles of mercy, but also to upset their comfort zones. In *care-fronting* the scribes and Pharisees, Jesus also lashed out, calling them "You hypocrites!...Let them alone; they are blind guides of the blind. And if one blind person guides another, both will fall into a pit" (Matt 15: 7, 14). He also rebuked them saying, "For you cross sea and land to make a single convert, twice as much a child of hell as yourselves" (Matt 23:15).

Jesus' message was not all sweetness; it was also challenging: "If another member of the church sins against you, go and point out the fault when the two of you are alone. If the member listens to you, you have regained that one. But if you are not listened to, take one or two others with you, so that every word may be confirmed by the evidence of two or three witnesses. If the member refuses to listen to them, tell it to the church; and if the offender refuses to listen even to the church, let such a one be to you as a Gentile and a tax collector" (Matt 18:15–17).

Scripture scholars can debate whether Jesus actually said this or not, especially the section concerning the church and how we are to treat individuals. However, we cannot argue against the need to go to someone who has wronged us rather than writing a letter or note. In some situations, the only way might be a letter or note, but too many of these have been misunderstood or misinterpreted. Face-to-face encounters can often settle what the written word cannot. How many of us are willing to do that? More often we prefer the easier way.

If this encounter fails, then we should seek the advice of a wise person to help us. There is strength in numbers. Deuteronomy states: "A single witness shall not suffice to convict a person of any crime or wrongdoing in connection with any offense that may be committed. Only on the evidence of two or three witnesses shall a charge be sustained" (Deut 19:15).

If this approach fails, according to Matthew's Gospel, we should take the matter to the fellowship of Christians where the situation may be judged in a spirit of love and prayer. Should this approach not produce any results, then we might regard the stubborn person no better than a tax collector or a Gentile. Even they can be forgiven, as was obvious from the lives of Zacchaeus and Matthew. So we don't ever abandon the person as hopeless, but continue to love the individual because as Saint Paul tells us, "Love never fails" (1 Cor 13:8).

When Jesus taught his apostles how much he was going to suffer, be rejected, and put to death and rise three days later, Peter took him aside and began to remonstrate with him saying that would never happen to him. Jesus *care-fronted* Peter with the words: "Get behind me, Satan! For you are not setting your mind on divine things but on human things" (Mark 8:33).

One day Philip said to Jesus: "Lord, show us the Father, and we will be satisfied." Jesus said to him, "Have I been with you all this time, Philip, and you still do not know me? Whoever has seen me has seen the Father" (John 14:8–9). Philip's statement probably hurt Jesus, but he *care-fronted* him and let him know what effect his mistrust had on him. Jesus shows us the importance of when to speak. Ecclesiastes states that there is "a time to keep silence, and a time to speak" (Eccl 3:7). Jesus knew when to speak and when to keep silent.

Purpose of *Care-frontation*

The purpose of *care-frontation* is not always meant to change the behavior of the other person. Rather it is to create an environment where it becomes possible for a person to change his or her behavior.[2] It presents the person being *care-fronted* with an opportunity for self examination. A powerful example of this is found in the Second Book of Samuel when Nathan *care-fronts* David. David had fallen in love with Bathsheba, but found out she was married to Uriah. Yet David had relations with her, and she told him later that she was with child. So David sent Uriah to the front lines, where he was killed.

After this, Nathan was sent by God to David to *care-front* him. He created the climate for change by telling him a story of a rich man and poor one. The rich man had huge herds and flocks. The poor man had nothing but a little lamb. The rich man entertained a visitor, but instead of using one of his own sheep to serve the visitor, he killed the poor man's only lamb. David got very upset and said to Nathan, "As the Lord lives, the man who has done this deserves to die!" Then Nathan said to David: "You are the man!" (2 Sam 12:5, 7). David reflected on what he had done and his repentance is graphically depicted in Psalm 51.

Jesus was a master at creating the climate for someone to change. He spotted Zacchaeus, the tax collector, in the sycamore tree and told him that he wanted to dine with him. Zacchaeus told Jesus: "Look, half of my possessions, Lord, I will give to the poor; and if I have defrauded anyone of anything, I will pay back four times as much" (Luke 19:8). Because of Jesus' willingness to dine with Zacchaeus, he and his whole household were converted.

In another situation, Jesus also *care-fronted* the Pharisee, Simon, who invited Jesus to dine with him. When a woman known to be a sinner appeared at the house, Simon could not understand how Jesus would allow her to bathe his feet with her tears and anoint them. Jesus told him, "I entered your house; you gave me no water for my feet, but she has bathed my feet with her tears and dried them with her hair. You gave me no kiss, but from the time I came in she has not stopped kissing my feet. You did not anoint my head with oil, but she has anointed my feet with ointment. Therefore, I tell you, her sins, which were many, have been forgiven; hence she has shown great love" (Luke 7:44–47).

When *care-fronting*, we have to make sure we are not trying to punish the person or group. It is easy to get even, seek revenge, or dominate a person or group by *care-fronting* them. When we have something painful to say, try to say it softly with words that heal and don't hurt so much. "Speaking the truth in love," Saint Paul advised the Ephesians (4:15). We must always remember that we are more interested in others' growth or creating a climate for them to change. Jesus did not lash out at the men who brought an adulteress to him. He calmly said to them: "Let anyone among you who is without sin, be the first to throw a stone at her" (John 8:7). Realizing their own sinfulness, they started to walk away. Jesus then gave the woman some sound advice: "Go your way and from now on do not sin again" (John 8:11).

Too often we *care-front* to relieve our frustrations or anxiety. Or we end up just telling off the person or group. This approach only increases the conflict or stress rather than diminishing or lessening it. At times we need not speak. The amazing part about Jesus was that when he spoke, his few words had such a tremendous impact on his listeners. The same was true when he kept silent. There is a saying, "never speak unless it is an improvement on silence."

In addition to creating a climate for change, another purpose of *care-frontation* is to offer the maximum amount of information with the minimum of threat and stress. Yet the opposite usually happens. Jesus said to the Samaritan woman: "Go, call your husband, and come back." The woman answered him, "I have no husband." Jesus said to her "You are right in saying, 'I have no husband'; for you have had five husbands, and the one you have now is not your husband. What you have said is true!" (John 4:16–18). Jesus' honesty and willingness to carry on the dialogue changed her life. She then influenced other Samaritans from that town to believe in Jesus. He led her from the fact that he was a male Jew to the realization that he was the Messiah. By this encounter with Jesus, she became a sharer of good news!

Forms of *Care-Frontation*

Too often conflict is dealt with in an indirect rather than a direct way. If someone really bothers us, we take a shower, go swimming, scrub the floor, or watch television instead of speaking to the person. Television can be a way to vent some of our feelings, especially by watching violence enacted. Wrestling or watching football can sometimes be a way to deal with our frustrations or hidden anger. I once saw someone who disagreed with a call a referee made during a football game go up to the television set with his fist upraised and cry: "That's wrong!"

We can also use verbal abuse to deal with a person or a group by means of cynicism, sarcasm, ridicule, or caustic, critical remarks. People working for their respective churches often are faced with the prospect of growing in their faith or becoming cynical. Often this is dealt with in one of two ways: either they decide to stay and hang in there with the church despite experiencing powerlessness, or they depart, drop out, pursuing other ventures such as guitar lessons, astrology, or psychiatry. One of the better ways to counteract someone else's cynicism is to have the courage to say something uplifting or humorous, rather than let the conversation deteriorate.

Saint Paul encourages us: "Let no evil talk come out of your mouths, but only what is useful for building up" (Eph 4:29). A priest was trying to encourage a certain woman to come back to the church. She responded, "You Catholics are nothing but hypocrites, hypocrites." After she kept on repeating this over and over again, the priest finally said to her, "Why don't you come back, there is always room for one more hypocrite!"

Too often we become sarcastic in dealing with *care-frontation*. Sarcasm can be very devastating because in getting a point across, it can injure another person's good reputation or make the person feel very uneasy. Some people are not even aware of how sarcastic they are. When *care-fronted* about our sarcasm, some of us will deny it or make excuses that we did not intend this. Above all, how many of us are willing or have the courage to leave when sarcastic remarks are made, or show the speaker some kind of disapproval?

Many snide remarks get traded at times concerning others or a situation. Verbal snipers take their potshots at others but make sure that we can't return the volley. Others are bulldozers who roll over us and hope that will do the job. Exploders really should have a sign over themselves: "Danger, high voltage!" The clammers won't speak at all, and if they do, it is "Nope," or "Yep." These and many other indirect ways of acting do not work. What we do not talk out, we will act out, but often we feel so powerless in talking to these people who bother us. We console ourselves by thinking that we don't want to "rock the boat" or that this is the "way they are and not much can be done about it."

However, the scriptures challenge us. If we read the first five chapters of the Acts of the Apostles, we are given the impression that everything was running very smoothly in the early church. We need to read on further because in Chapter Six, we discover how the widows who spoke Greek complained because they were being neglected in the daily distribution of food. The twelve gathered together and addressed the problem by selecting seven men filled with the spirit to take care of the situation. In Chapter Fifteen, we read how Barnabas wanted to take Mark along on a trip. Paul refused because Mark had deserted them at Pamphylia. The disagreement became so acute that Paul and Barnabas went their separate ways. However, Paul and Mark later were reconciled.

Saint Paul often had to *care-front* the early church, especially in Corinth: "Now in the following instructions I do not commend you, because when you come together it is not for the better but for the worse. For, to begin with, when you come together as a church, I hear that there are divisions among you; and to some extent I believe it" (1 Cor 11:17–18). Paul knew what to expect at times: "For I fear that when I come, I may find you not as I wish, and that you may find me not as you wish; I fear that there may perhaps be quarreling, jealousy, anger, selfishness, slander, gossip, conceit, and disorder" (2 Cor 12:20).

Has the church today changed that much? What would Paul write to *us?* I know of a parish where the associate pastor had a weekly column in the parish bulletin. He used a clever approach to get his point across by writing that his dog noticed how people were coming late and leaving early from church. Needless to say, his column was well read. Why were people able to receive this message? Was this a modern form of parable? Or were they enamored by the way it was done?

When *care-fronted* we will often find escapes or make excuses. We are wired with a flight-or-fight response. Some ward off the *care-frontation* by defending themselves with responses such as "I have always been this way." "Sorry, this is the way I am." "I was like this in the beginning, am now, and ever shall be." Probably the best answer is "Then, nature has done badly."

Others will attack the *care-fronter* saying: "You do the same thing." That often leaves us in a powerless position if it is true, but it still needs to be said. We can also procrastinate and hope we won't have to *care-front* because maybe the person will change. So we keep on tolerating the behavior or the situation, which usually becomes much worse. This explains why some people become set in their ways.

Sometimes we would like someone else to *care-front* the individual, especially someone in authority like a local leader or boss. The problem often boils down to how we deal with difficult people. Or, put another way, how do we embrace a porcupine? Too often these people will not even let you get close to them or allow us to say much to them. However, as Christians we do not give up if we care and love enough.

Manner of *Care-Fronting*

If *care-fronting* means that we are interested in another's growth, we need to pray over the matter before engaging in this delicate act of communication. We have to make sure we don't put ourselves in an "I win—you lose" situation. If we are honest with ourselves, we know how biased we can become toward someone else. If we are, we have to know it is not easy to tell the person about these biases. It can be very challenging to speak to the person as an equal, not as someone inferior to us. The gospels make it evidently clear how Jesus spoke to others in this way; he showed and demonstrated a radical mutuality. He did not consider himself better than they were, even though he was sinless.

When *care-fronting* others we have to be careful not to do it out of revenge, punishment, domination, or a desire to shame the person. It is easy to fall into this trap. Even though Jesus called the scribes and Pharisees hypocrites, he did not lash out at them in a spirit of revenge or punishment. Although it is easy to shame someone, especially before others, this can be most humiliating and often accomplishes little if any good.

I remember when I was a young seminarian, my pastor and I drove to Huntington, Indiana, from Wisconsin. He asked me to drive part of the way. At the time I was still learning how to drive. I passed a car and he asked me: "Do you mind if I make a suggestion?" I responded, "No, go ahead." He instructed me: "When you pass a car you have to make sure you have really passed the car before pulling back into the lane." I never forgot that, especially the manner in which he told me. He didn't say, "You dumb klotz, don't you know what you just did?" When we have something painful to say, try to use this approach. Once the person agrees to the suggestion, you have an opening.

Blaming a person only evokes a lot of resistance and resentment. Experts point out how blame is powerless to affect any true change and growth. From the beginning, Adam blamed Eve and Eve blamed the serpent. We all have our own guilt and have a tendency to blame ourselves. Robert Hoffman has written the book *No One Is to Blame*, in which he maintains that we are all guilty to some extent, but no one is to blame.[3] Until we learn this nugget of truth there is very little possibility of change. We might not be culpable for the evils in the world that we often deplore, but we are still responsible because we are all interconnected. My sin, especially social sin, does affect others. This message is a difficult pill to swallow.

In *care-fronting* a person, we need to focus on the behavior or motivation and not make an attack on the person. Jesus pointed out the behavior of the scribes and Pharisees: "They tie up heavy burdens hard to bear, and lay them on the shoulders of others; but they themselves are unwilling to lift a finger to move them. They do all their deeds to be seen by others; for they make their phylacteries broad and their fringes long. They love to have the place of honor at banquets and the best seats in the synagogues..." (Matt 23:4–7). Can some of these words apply to us as well?

When *care-fronting* someone, we need to be careful to state what is fact and what is feeling. Too many feelings can be expressed in a condemning or judgmental way. For example, when asking someone for information, we might receive a grunt, groan, or silence in reply. So we might ask: "Please tell me what that groan, grunt or silence mean?"

It is also important to deal with one problem at a time, not a whole litany of grievances. The tendency is to unload on the person, or to remember misdeeds that have happened many years ago. Very often, the person won't be able to remember or is too emotional to accept more than one problem. When we complain about something, for example, a place left dirty, we have to make sure that this really is the problem, not just a cover for a deeper problem, such as an inability to relate to the person.

Also allow the person or group to give some feedback to make sure we are understood. Too often we can *care-front* the person or group and then even ask in a domineering way, "Are there any questions?" and receive no answer because the person and group do not feel free to reply. Allowing the person or group to give us feedback ensures that we are understood. It shows if clarification is needed or if there was a misinterpretation of what was said.

It is important to *care-front* immediately and not to wait or procrastinate. Procrastination has often been characterized as the devil's chloroform. The devil really is not concerned how much we do, as long as we don't do it today. Not *care-fronting* immediately only makes it a tough job later. We have to join the TNT club: Today Not Tomorrow. Some time ago, I was told by a friend how I should have pointed out immediately a behavior that upset me rather than wait a few days. The suggestion was appropriate and remembered.

Parents sometimes delay. They need to teach their children at an early age the difference between *care-frontation* and an attack, as well as fairness and accountability. Children will feel more secure and protected if they are treated with fairness. They need the help of a parent or a teacher when they are involved in a *care-*

frontation situation. It can be very devastating to a child for parents or a teacher to ignore a reported need. "Don't be a tattle tale," often is not sound advice. Mediating the children together in a loving, caring manner often leads to apologies, handshakes, and even hugs. Home and school can become safe havens where better relationships and fair exchanges can take place.

Not everyone, however, is capable of *care-fronting* others in a helpful way. Brother Juniper, who was known as "the little clown of God," helped Saint Francis of Assisi from becoming too serious. Because he was so guileless, Juniper was able to correct his brothers without any of them taking offense. No wonder Saint Francis wished that he had a forest of Junipers.

Self *Care-Frontation*

We need to *care-front* ourselves at times. Saint Augustine admitted in his *Confessions* that he had wasted twelve years of his life, and one of the biggest obstacles was his sexual relationships. He wanted chastity and self-control but not right away, so he kept putting off his conversion. So much of our lifetime, we play hide and seek with God.

Catherine Doherty, foundress of the Madonna House Apostolate, maintained that we sit on the fence of compromise. We need conversion, as Andrew Costello points out in his book *How to Deal with Difficult People,* which tells us how many people were converted by Jesus.[4] Saint Paul admonishes us, "Now is the acceptable time; see, now is the day of salvation" (2 Cor 6:2).

At times we need to *care-front* our shadow or parts of ourselves we fail to recognize. "Know thyself" is still solid advice, but there might be feelings or desires we are too ashamed to admit or have repressed even from childhood. Because our tendency is to deny or reject our shadow, we might project it on others. So what we find distasteful, annoying, or even hateful in others could be also true of ourselves. These characteristics become more evident when we are tired, harassed, irritated, or under some other form of stress. Christians readily admit how difficult a task it is to *care-front* their shadow but acknowledge how this can lead to a better understanding of oneself and help us to grow in the spiritual life.

Benefits of *Care-frontation*

The benefits of *care-frontation* cannot be overemphasized. It is a vital skill that can and should be developed and improved by all Christians. One of the benefits is the ability to ease the tension and conflict that often arises between individuals or in groups. Without *care-frontation* the tension and conflict continue to grow, and matters get worse or deteriorate. In the early church, conflicts regarding circumcision were time consuming. After much discussion, especially between Peter and Paul, they decided that the Gentiles need not be circumcised. Paul encouraged the Ephesians "speaking the truth in love, we must grow up in every way into him who is the head, into Christ" (Eph 4:15). *Care-frontation* ensures the possibility of a successful resolution.

Care-frontation is a powerful way to build healthy relationships that are necessary for development. It is a way to help us out of mediocrity and prod us on to more growth. We need to make others feel important like Jesus did, and to take them as they are, not as we want them to be. Solomon, when asked what he wanted from God, did not ask for wisdom but an understanding heart. That is indeed a precious gift and one needed to *care-front* others. The result will help us to better grasp how we can't relate to others in the same way. Words may fail us at times, but love will bridge whatever gap is there.

Patrick Brennan in his book *Paschal Journey* writes: "I think that there might be more enduring relationships, healthier people, less compulsive self destructive behavior if more of us learned to gently confront, challenge, intervene, rather than ignoring dysfunctional behavior, engaging in avoidance behaviors, or sweeping obvious problems under the rug."[5]

Care-frontation is an important facet of communication. This kind of communication can bring us closer to others, and this closeness will help us grow as persons. We are most a person when we communicate effectively. Our growth is dependent on our contact with others, and the deeper the contact the greater growth will result. *Care-frontation,* however, requires risk and pain involved in the encounter. However, the results can be most gratifying, especially to help clear the air and to express our feelings, which can deepen and improve our relationships with others. Isn't this the real goal of *care-frontation?*

It has been proven that those who exert the most influence in organizations are those best equipped to handle *care-frontation.* *Care-frontation* can help us to know ourselves and others better, and to value more the gift of friendship. Paul wrote to the Colossians: "Let your speech always be gracious seasoned with salt..." (Col 4:6). Wise advice for any *care-fronter.*

※　※　※

SCRIPTURE PASSAGES FOR REFLECTION

"A single witness shall not suffice to convict a person of any crime or wrongdoing in connection with any offense that may be committed.

Only on the evidence of two or three witnesses shall a charge be sustained." (Deut 19:15)

"A time to keep silence, and a time to speak." (Eccl 3:7)

"You are the man!" (2 Sam 12:7)

"Love never fails" (1 Cor 13:8)

"Speaking the truth in love" (Eph 4:15)

QUESTIONS TO CONSIDER

1. How do you think that Jesus would *care-front* us today?

2. Why do I find it hard to *care-front*—fear, insecurity, anger of others?

3. How can I create more of a climate for others to change?

4. Where do I need to *care-front* myself?

5. Do I have an understanding heart, and if so, how is it shown?

7

HOW FORGIVING
ARE WE?

"Father, forgive them, for they do not know what they are doing"
Luke 23:34

Christians often pride themselves in how giving they are, especially to charitable organizations. Indeed, many are but we
need to *care-front* ourselves asking, "How forgiving are we?"

Actually, forgiveness is looked down upon in our society or
culture; we often are considered a wimp or weak if we forgive.
That is contrary to what Jesus taught and preached. Peter asked
Jesus how often he had to forgive—seven times? For a Jew to forgive someone twice was commendable, so Peter probably figured
if he could triple that number and add one, which is the perfect
number, that ought to be sufficient. Jesus responded, "Not seven
times, but, I tell you, seventy-seven times" (Matt 18:22). Does
that mean once we reach the magic number of 490, that's it? No,
it means that we have to continue to forgive over and over again,
not counting the times. Now that is most challenging for any
Christian.

Some Christians will say that they are willing to forgive, provided the other party apologizes first. If this attitude prevails,
then we really do not understand the highest kind of love that

always takes the initiative. God did not have to create this world, but he did out of love. Adam and Eve, once they sinned, never said that they were sorry, but God took the initiative and sent us the Father's most precious gift of Jesus. Ruth Burrows, a British Carmelite, stated it well in *Living the Mystery*, noting God gave us all God could give us in Jesus. God kept nothing back, not even God's only precious Son, and that was the gift of divine Self.

To demand that others must first apologize to us is demanding more than Jesus did. Jesus took the initiative by reaching out to sinners and outcasts as well as people who needed healing. He did not say to the woman caught in adultery, "What else did you do?" He said to the men, "'Let anyone among you who is without sin be the first to throw a stone at her.' And once again he bent down and wrote on the ground. When they heard it, they went away, one by one, beginning with the elders; and Jesus was left alone with the woman standing before him. Jesus straightened up and said to her, 'Woman, where are they? Has no one condemned you?' She said, 'No one, sir.' And Jesus said, 'Neither do I condemn you. Go your way, and from now on do not sin again'" (John. 8:7–11).

To Simon, who invited Jesus to dine with him, Jesus said of the sinful woman, "Therefore, I tell you, her sins, which were many, have been forgiven; hence she has shown great love" (Luke 7:47).

To the good thief on the cross he said, "Truly, I tell you, today you will be with me in Paradise" (Luke 23:43).

Lack of Forgiveness

The lack of forgiveness can eat away at us like a cancer so that we can become even more angry and resentful, like the elder son in the prodigal son story. This parable really should be called the prodigal father story because it is the father who takes the initiative and is waiting for his son to return. When he sees him at a distance, the father is filled with compassion and runs to greet his lost son, embracing and kissing him. He then tells his servants to put the finest robe on his son, a ring on his finger, sandals on his feet, and to kill the fatted calf so all could celebrate. However, the elder son becomes angry and will not come in the house.

Many of us can identify with the elder son. A teacher told this story to a group of small children and when she finished, she asked the children, "Now of all the characters in this story, whom do you feel sorry for the most?" She was hoping one of them would say the elder son. Finally, a hand shot up and the child said, "I feel sorry for the fatted calf the most."

One of the most effective ways of dealing with anger or resentment is to learn to forgive. Forgiveness is not easy because it involves all our faculties: mind, emotions, memory, and will. Some people think that the anger will disappear once we forgive, but this is often a slow process, and we might find ourselves angry again. Forgiveness happens when we divest ourselves of self-destructive emotions, such as a desire for revenge. We do not need, however, to verbalize the forgiveness because it is an inner transformation. Authentic forgiveness is not a business deal; it has to be given with no strings attached. Saint Paul reminds us, " just as the Lord has forgiven you, so you also must forgive" (Col 3:13).

Why do we hang onto anger or resentment? Well, actually, there are secondary gains involved. Anger can protect us from more painful or fearful emotions like loneliness or sadness. It can be a cover up for our own inadequacy. Additionally, anger supplies energy, whereas sadness and depression make us more helpless and hopeless. Anger can also keep others at a distance. If we fear intimacy, one of the best defenses is anger. Anger can gain attention, especially a temper tantrum or a tirade, and is a powerful way to control others or to be in charge, compensating for our powerlessness.

However, forgiveness can give us a sense of greater power as is brought out by the rabbi who was a survivor of the Holocaust and came to this country. He said that he refused to bring Hitler with him. What a contrast to Jonah who was asked by God if he had a reason to be angry. What is Jonah angry about? A gourd plant that grew up and provided shade for him withered and died. Jonah responded, "Yes, angry enough to die" (Jonah 4:9). The amazing part of this book is that it just ends there. We don't know if Jonah ever resolves his unjust anger. How many Christians never resolve their unjust anger, holding onto it like a crutch, or, worse yet, dying with it.

In his State of the Union Address in 2006, President Bush stated that we cannot allow our differences to harden into anger. Lack of restoration to civility definitely will have very serious consequences. Resentment is comparable to harboring a thief in our hearts. It steals our joy and robs us of our energy. Many people lug around resentment that acts as a burden weighing them down. Resentment is like CD headphones continuously playing poisonous messages in our minds.

Forgiveness is a giver whereas anger and resentment are takers. Forgiveness has been described as pulling the knife out of our own gut. It frees the employee who was passed over for a promotion, a relative who might not have been invited to a wedding, or an ex-spouse who harbors bitter feelings toward a former spouse. At times, the other person might not even be aware of our resentment. While bitterness eats away at them, the person who hurt them doesn't feel anything.

There is a story about a couple who were arguing most of the day, and finally because they were so angry and resentful, they stopped speaking to each other. The husband remembered that he had an important meeting the next day. The wife was an early riser, but he, refusing to be the first one to give in, wrote her a note asking her to make sure he got up at 5 a.m. He put the note on her pillow and went to bed. The next morning he woke up and to his horror it was 7 a.m. Furious, he got out of bed and spotted a note on his nightstand. It read: It's 5 a.m. Time to get up! Anger leads to further spiraling of anger.

Why do we hang onto anger and even hatred? It might be a way to protect ourselves from further hurt, to avoid dealing with a deeper hurt, or to escape a sense of emptiness there. Once we let go, we become loving persons, and it will fill the emptiness and void. Self-giving moves us away from ourselves to others like homebound people or disabled children. We become healthier and live more meaningful lives.

The Example of Jesus

Jesus gave us the powerful example of how we should forgive. When Peter had told Jesus that he would die with him, Jesus predicted that Peter would deny him three times, which Peter did. So what did Jesus say to Peter? Not a single word. He gives him a loving glance of forgiveness and Peter weeps bitterly for what he had done. More loving glances rather than hateful glares are needed.

Jesus also forgave Judas, who betrayed him for thirty pieces of silver. What does Jesus say to Judas? "You rat fink! How could you do this to me?" No, he calls him "friend." Now if Jesus was just as human as anyone of us he certainly had many deep-seated feelings about Judas.

His Holiness of happy memory, Pope John Paul II, was shot in Saint Peter's Square in 1981. Later the Pope visited his would be assassin, Ali Agca, in prison and forgave him. In another act of forgiveness, Cardinal Joseph Bernardin was falsely accused of sodomy by Steven Cook in 1996. Cook later recanted. They met and prayed together and were reconciled. Or consider the stunning example of the Amish families in Nickel Mines, Pennsylvania, who sent words of forgiveness to the family of the killer who executed their ten children.

Probably one of the most powerful stories that I recall reading happened in Russia. A Russian mother saw her only son killed by a soldier. One day as she was walking in the street, she came across a man lying in the ditch. She could tell that he was dying. Upon looking closer at him, she recognized that he was the soldier who killed her son. She nursed him back to life and adopted him as her son. How many of us would be willing to do that or something comparable?

Some Christians continue to carry grudges, ill will toward others, or negative feelings. They even hold a rosary in one hand and a grudge in another, and don't see the inconsistency. Then they wonder why their prayers are not answered.

Grudges strip our hearts. They are comparable to a black hole that sucks out our vital energy, making us prisoners of our own hearts. It takes much emotional and psychological energy to keep a grudge alive. Nursing grudges will never make them better. It is also comparable to a wound that we allow to fester or one that we keep picking away at until the wound becomes worse.

In Mark's Gospel we read, "Herodias had a grudge against him [John the Baptist] and wanted to kill him. But she could not, for Herod feared John" (Mark 6:19). We know the rest of the story, how she finally succeeded in telling her daughter to ask for the head of John the Baptist. It is a powerful story pointing out the need to let go of our grudges and pray for healing.

Some time ago, I came across an article entitled "Three Words that Heal." You might guess what they are: "I forgive you." Healing will take place to the extent that we let go of our grudges and hurts and forgive others.

Hurts

Why do we Christians find it hard to forgive at times? One of the reasons is because of the hurt that is involved. We see everything through a prism of pain and injury. Hurts can cut very deeply and often prevent us from forgiving. I can remember as a grade-school child that I worked for a man who paid me fifty cents a week. He would pay me at the end of the week once he inspected my work. One time he threw the fifty-cent piece on the ground and I had to pick it up. I don't know why he did this, but I cried all the way home, and it took me a long time to forgive him.

When I was in eighth grade, I decided that I wanted to become a priest. So I told my teacher, who was a Franciscan Sister. I never got along with her, so she responded, "You'll never make it." However, that provided even more incentive! What a contrast to Father George Henseler, a Capuchin priest, who interviewed me before joining the Capuchins. I told him that I didn't know if I could make it because I didn't know much about the Capuchins. He gave me one of his piercing looks and said emphatically, "You'll make it!"

After ordination, I conducted a retreat for those same Franciscan Sisters, and guess who was on this retreat? I am almost certain she was strutting around saying, "And I had him in grade school." It is also customary to sign up for a private conference with the retreat master. She did this and I said to myself, "Ah, here is my opportunity, to plan my little Pearl Harbor attack and get back at her." However, through God's grace I resisted. What I had to learn was that no one can hurt us unless we allow the person to do this. We must make the decision to take the moral high ground and forget the jingle, "Do unto others before they do it unto you."

My hurts, however, pale into insignificance when I consider what some Christians have to suffer and endure. I remember a woman on a retreat that I was conducting who had been sexually abused by her father. She told me how she could not forgive him. In the course of that retreat, the Spirit touched her so deeply that she finally forgave him. That became the turning point in her life, and what a heavy burden was lifted from her.

Our greatest hurt, whatever that might be, has to become our greatest blessing, not our greatest curse. For many Christians their greatest hurt has become their greatest curse. They find it hard to forgive or let go. How can this happen?

Again we look to the scriptures. Joseph was undoubtedly hurt by his brothers when they sold him into Egypt. However, after his struggle and various maneuvers, he forgave them by saying, "I am your brother Joseph, whom you sold into Egypt. And now do not be distressed, or angry with yourselves because you sold me here; for God sent me before you to preserve life" (Gen. 45:4–5). His greatest hurt became Egypt's greatest blessing.

Consider Jesus: what do you think caused him the most suffering in his passion? Some will say the crowning with thorns, others the scourging, and still others the three-hour agony on the cross. One theologian believes that what caused Jesus the most suffering was when the people scoffed at him and cried out, "You who would destroy the temple and build it in three days, save yourself! If you are the Son of God, come down from the cross. In the same way the chief priests also, along with the scribes and elders, were mocking him saying, 'He saved others; he cannot save himself'" (Matt 27:40–42). Jesus said, "Father, forgive them, for they do not know what they are doing" (Luke 23:34). Jesus' greatest hurt, whatever it was, became our greatest blessing. This is the challenge that he offers us if we are truly his followers and proclaim that we are Christians. We need to be magnanimous to forgive a deep hurt.

Some of us possess what might be called a Velcro personality where all our hurts stick—this happened two, five, or twenty years ago. These emotional hurts or wounds become like fish bones stuck in our throats. Spouses have a tendency to remind each other how they were deeply hurt in the past. In comparison, others are fortunate in having a Teflon personality where the hurts slide off very easily. That comes with the ability to let go of the hurts, stop playing the tapes, and especially cease picking away at the scabs. These people, like Jesus, have forgiving eyes that take the place of words. I remember reading that a famous astronomer stated that the moon is actually the size of an orange when held at arm's length. Hurts held closely definitely warp our perspective, so we need to see people who have hurt us with new eyes, the eyes of Jesus.

Break the Cycle

Therapists maintain that a lack of forgiveness or unfinished business can afflict families through seven generations unless there is some resolution. The key is not to pass on the hurt or pain but to break the cycle.

Some years ago I received a letter from a lady who attended a parish renewal that I had conducted. She wrote, "You can take great pride in being the source of my courage to repair differences my eldest son and I have had. After Wednesday's sermon on forgiveness, I came home and made a long overdue call, and my animosity has vanished. Love abides once again." God's word does touch lives. Jesus became man to show us how to do this. God doesn't take away the pain but joins us in the suffering. Jesus was willing to lay down his own life that we might have life to the fullest.

A plan to aid us in forgiveness might be to practice forgiving small hurts, such as the person who cuts us off while driving, the store clerk who shortchanges us, a waitress who might be gruff, a loved one or a coworker who answers with a harsh word. It bolsters what Jesus said about being faithful in small things to prepare us for the greater one. We often need to vent our anger or resentment to a trusted friend or spiritual director. Just hearing ourselves can be a healing experience. Write the person a letter without blaming the person and then either send it or tear it up.

The advice to just forget what has happened is not wise or prudent. How is it possible for someone who has experienced something traumatic like a rape, an abortion, a mugging, a divorce, a stillbirth, to just forget it? That is not possible unless one receives a special grace from God. We are able to pull chips out of the memory of a computer, but it is far more difficult to just forget or delete something from our brain. Jesus never forgot his passion and death.

Rabbi Abraham Heschel insisted that nothing could be learned if we forgot the Holocaust. Where was a loving God at Auschwitz? Did God remain silent, as Pope Benedict XVI asked recently on his visit there? Because the Jews are the chosen race, is this their fate? How can such inhumanity of gas chambers and ovens be conceived? If I were a survivor of the Holocaust, would I be able to forgive? We must not forget injustices but deal with them appropriately.

I remember a woman telling me that going through a divorce was worse than death. What needs to be done is not to keep on recalling the event or becoming entangled in its tentacles. Otherwise we keep on drinking the vinegar of revenge, anger, and bitterness. What we need to do is pour on the balm of Gilead (Gen 37:25; Jer 8:22). Gilead is a place known for its aromatic perfume:

> There is a balm in Gilead
> to make the wounded whole.
> There is a balm in Gilead
> to heal the sin-sick soul.[1]

The balm now is the Holy Spirit. To forgive is definitely God's grace in action and is often called the eighth gift of the Holy Spirit. It might not come immediately; it takes time. There is no easy fix. The person who gains most is the person who forgives.

Forgiving Oneself

Some Christians maintain that they are able to forgive others, but they have a hard time forgiving themselves. They continually live in the past and allow what has happened there to haunt them. If we live in the past, we often live with much guilt, and that probably explains why we have many guilt-ridden Christians. If we live in the future we live with slavish fear. That is the teeter-totter syndrome that many of us are prone to fall into.

Consider for a moment how much of our time is taken up with either the past or the future. We are robbing the present moment, and that is all we have. The last minute is gone, and the next minute is not here. As Christians we have to live the *now* and that will change our lives.

Our true identity is found in the present moment. This becomes more evident in death, which strips away all that doesn't belong to us. "The secret of life," according to Eckhart Tolle, a counselor and spiritual teacher, "is to 'die before you die,' and to find that there is no death."[2] Saint Paul expressed it well, "Death has been swallowed up in victory. Where, O death, is your victory? Where, O death, is your sting?" (1 Cor 15:5).

God has more readily forgiven us of our past than we have. Why are we so hard on ourselves? We need to pray each day to forgive ourselves and give the past into the hands of a loving, forgiving, compassionate God. God's forgiveness is rooted in unconditional love, a love that has no strings attached and is boundless, as we have seen.

Jennifer O'Neill, a famous actress, had an abortion in the early 70's. She maintains in her book *From Fallen to Forgiven* that no matter what we might have done, God forgives. How true. She thanks God for how she is being used to help other women who have suffered the emotional pain of abortion. As noted in her book, she believes that 43 percent of women over the age of 55 have had an abortion. She continues to help others to forgive themselves.

The inability to forgive ourselves is sometimes linked to the fear of narcissism, according to some experts. Narcissistic people usually have low self-esteem and they are unable to cope with injuries or slights. They find it hard to forgive wrongs or slights done to them, and they make it almost impossible to forgive themselves if they have harmed others. Their cross in many instances is perfectionism. These individuals can overcome these tendencies with proper guidance and thereby live a healthier life.

One of the signs that the individual is making progress in this area is a sense of humor. Pope John XXIII had a marvelous sense of humor. One day someone asked him, "How many people work for you here in the Roman Curia? His immediate response was, "About half of them." We have to learn to laugh at our mistakes and not take life so seriously. Developing a good sense of humor takes the sting out of the harsh realities we all face in life. The awareness of God's presence and unconditional love also helps immensely, for God has not destined us for wrath but for peace.

Jeremiah is a good example of someone who expected God's backing, support, and love. Instead he felt abandonment and suffered insult and injury. He went so far as to say, "You enticed me, and I was enticed; you have overpowered me, and you have prevailed. I have become a laughingstock all day long; everyone mocks me" (Jer 20:7). However, God was with him when he least expected it and experienced "something like burning fire shut up in my bones; I am weary with holding it in, and I cannot" (Jer 20:9).

We often have to lower our expectations and face the raw realities of life. Job also suffered very intensely and had to come to the realization that God was with him. He struggled a long time before he could understand how God is greater than our expectations.

After the 2004 tsunami struck, Ari Afrizai, from Indonesia, spent two weeks drifting on a raft in the Indian Ocean, surviving on coconuts. He was almost ready to give up hope, but he said that he didn't get angry because he was thankful to be alive. He maintained that just as heat and cold come from God, so also do life and death.

Benefits

The benefits of forgiveness cannot be overemphasized. It is freeing. Jesus told us that the truth will make us free. We definitely will have more peace of mind and heart because the walls of anger, resentment, and grudges will come tumbling down.[3] We also can become wounded healers helping others who have resisted forgiveness by telling them of our struggles. It definitely will help us lead healthier lives, reduce the stress on our heart, avoid high blood pressure and ulcers, and lessen the possibility for other diseases. Forgiveness will enable us to continue as pilgrims on our spiraling journey toward God. It will enable us to carry on the work of Jesus, whose life exemplified forgiveness.

Forgiveness can have cosmic effects. Imagine what could happen if nations and religious groups or sects were willing to put aside all their animosities. It could be the key to the survival of our planet. We could alter the face of the earth.

There is a story about some monkeys on a South Pacific island who loved to eat sweet potatoes. When they ate them, they hated to get the dirt and sand in their mouths. One monkey, however, got smart and washed his potato. Others noticed this and did the same. Scientists have proven how this idea spread to the other islands in the Pacific. The same could be true if just one person forgave and, this in turn, influenced others to do the same.

Forgiveness of others can have a ripple effect. When others see us as forgiving Christians, they can be inspired to also forgive. The fact that we hold hands during the Our Father or offer a handshake of peace to others does not make us Christians; forgiveness does.

A good example is Robin Casarjian, who relates how she was able to forgive the man who raped her in *Forgiveness: A Bold Choice for a Peaceful Heart.* She maintains that once we forgive, we are no longer handcuffed by that person. What a different world could be created if everyone was willing to forgive others and oneself as Jesus forgave. Forgiveness remains the challenge for any Christian who has been deeply hurt. Forgiving others and ourselves becomes the litmus test in finding out what kind of Christian we are.

卝 卝 卝

SCRIPTURE PASSAGES FOR REFLECTION

"Not seven times, but, I tell you, seventy-seven times." (Matt 18:22)

"Let anyone among you who is without sin be the first to throw a stone at her." (John 8:7)

"I tell you, her sins, which were many, have been forgiven; hence she has shown great love." (Luke 7:47)

"Just as the Lord has forgiven you, so you also must forgive." (Col 3:13)

"For I will be merciful toward their iniquities, and I will remember their sins no more." (Heb 8:12)

QUESTIONS TO CONSIDER

1. What do we find ourselves demanding of another before forgiving the individual?

2. Do we find ourselves hanging onto anger, resentment, or a grudge?

3. What is our greatest hurt and has it become a curse or a blessing?

4. What has helped us in the process of forgiveness?

5. Have we found it difficult to forgive ourselves and why?

8

IS ATTITUDE
EVERYTHING?

"Who, though he was in the form of God,
    did not regard equality with God
    as something to be exploited,
but emptied himself,
    taking the form of a slave,
    being born in human likeness."
                                Phil 2:6–7

To be able to forgive others and ourselves demands that we possess a positive attitude toward life. Recently I saw a bumper sticker that read: "Attitude is everything."[1] There is much truth in that statement, especially for the Christian. The importance of a positive attitude cannot be overstated. Attitude is what others see in us, or hear in our voice, or feel in our presence. Our attitude expresses itself in everything we do or are as Christians.

What is attitude? It is a mental position with regard to a fact or statement. Our attitude will determine our potential, help us to be actively involved in projects, and predict good results. It directs us to perceive the events in our world and will determine our future as well as help us to face our challenges. It is basic to our daily living and forms the grist of our beliefs because often we straddle the border between belief and unbelief. Our lives are determined more by our beliefs than anything else. Our thoughts are the springboard of our attitudes and will form our thinking. Anthony Robbins, author of *Unlimited Power*, maintains that attitudes are at the epicenter, the core, of all human actions.

Attitudes have been compared to magnets pulling us as surely as a compass needle points in a certain direction. Our attitudes have been described as our self-fulfilling prophecies. Charles Swindoll, the famous author and lecturer, maintains that the longer he lives the more he realizes how important attitude is. He considers attitude to have a greater impact than facts, the past, education, money, circumstances, failures, successes, and even what people think or say about us. For him it is far more important than one's appearance, giftedness, or skills. In the final analysis, he believes it will break a company, a church, or a home. We might also add our lives. Attitude needs more of our attention and deeper reflection.

Reflection

People will often reflect to us the attitudes we project in a business, workplace, parish, or home. If we are cheerful, they are cheerful. We receive what we put out. If we possess a great attitude, we will produce great results. A good attitude achieves good results. A poor attitude produces poor results. This sounds so simple, but many things that appear simple are not easy.

Too many of our endeavors start in neutral or are very listless and apathetic. We need high octane at times. A high school teacher wrote the word *apathy* on the board in big bold letters. One student asked another student, "What's that?" The other responded, "Who cares?"

We sometimes say, "Who cares?" or "What's the use?" We cannot do much about a difficult situation, so we become resigned to mediocrity, indifference, or stagnation. The Book of Revelation records the following words addressed to the Laodiceans: "I know your works; you are neither cold nor hot. I wish you were either cold or hot. So, because you are lukewarm, and neither cold or hot, I am about to spit you out of my mouth" (Rev. 3:15). Could this passage also be addressed to us?[2]

Christians with a positive attitude take themselves seriously, especially who they are because they know that affects what they do. What we do in our daily lives affects who we become. We become what we do habitually, so if we drive like a maniac we become maniacs; if we respect others, we become more respectful. Habits, as we know, are much more difficult to change once they become part of us. It is much easier to acquire a habit than to change it. A good attitude and proper motivation are necessary because there is much resistance to overcome fits of anger and temper tantrums, which often indicate negative attitudes.

Negative Attitudes

Nothing is more detrimental to a Christian than a negative attitude. We have negative indicators in our cars for the battery and water and oil pressure but we don't keep looking at them. Frustration often arises in our lives and becomes a negative attitude. It usually is accompanied by excessive and emotional feelings, by a deep dissatisfaction and futility with life that leads to failure.

We often fail because of a Jonah complex. Jonah had a negative attitude toward going to Nineveh because he was convinced the people would not repent. Even when they converted, Jonah became angry and frustrated. God asks Jonah a very penetrating question, "Is it right for you to be angry?" What was Jonah angry about? A gourd plant that grew up and gave him shade, relieving him of any discomfort, suddenly withers and dies. Jonah cries out, "It is better for me to die than to live" (Jonah 4:4, 8). The book ends with God telling Jonah how the people of Nineveh are more important than a gourd plant. We also have to remember that advice.

Whenever a similar question is asked in the scriptures, it might be a question we need to ask of ourselves. When God asked Adam and Eve once they had sinned, "Where are you?" (Gen 3:9), it is a question we need to ask: Where are we in relationship to God, others, and ourselves? When Jesus asks the central question in the gospels, "Who do people say that the Son of Man is?" (Matt 6:13), we need to ask ourselves over and over again: Who is Jesus Christ in our lives? What is our response?

Closely linked to frustration is excessive aggressiveness, when we direct our energy by taking it out on others. It is similar to a certain scorpion in South America that will sting and kill itself with its poison when angered. Our aggressiveness is often not addressed personally or in meetings, but left to linger and poison ourselves. We need to find ways to express our aggressiveness in positive ways and not let it fester.

Cain became so aggressive that he killed Abel because Abel's offering was accepted by God and his was not. When God asked, "Where is your brother, Abel?" Cain said, "I do not know; am I my brother's keeper?" (Gen 4:9). Is that our response also? True Christians take who they are seriously because they realize that it affects what they do.

Some of us have become masters of negative strokes, criticism, and disdain for others. We will justify our actions by stating that they're wrong and we're right. We are fond of punishing others, wishing to silence them. Our response to creative ideas or new projects is that they won't work. Some delight in taking pot-shots at others as long as they don't receive any in return. They can walk through a cesspool and think that they don't stink. Everyone else does.

People with a negative attitude grumble and complain a lot. The Israelites grumbled and complained because of a steady diet of manna, so God sent them the quail. Still they were not satisfied. In the New Testament, Saint Paul encouraged the Philippians, "Do all things without murmuring or arguing" (Phil 2:14). Saint James encouraged his community, "Do not grumble against one another, so that you may not be judged" (Jas 5:9).

Some people seem unhappy unless they are complaining. They can be characterized as CCC people: Constant Chronic Complainers. The weather is too warm or too cold. One chronic complainer can bring down a whole work department. Some students complain about too much homework, the food in the cafeteria, or their seat in the classroom. One way a certain person dealt with chronic complainers was to listen to his litany of complaints and then said, "That sounds terrible. How do you deal with all those problems?" The response was, "It's not *that* bad!"

Attitude toward Self

Our attitudes toward ourselves can also be rather negative. We sometimes don't see anything good about ourselves, and often don't like the way we look. Remember the last time you had your picture taken and got the proofs back. What was your reaction?

There is much self-hatred within each one of us. With so much emphasis on external beauty, it is easy for that self-hatred to surface. Golda Meir, as a young girl, was discouraged because she was not beautiful. As she grew older, her attitude changed, and her lack of beauty became a blessing in disguise. She began to develop her inner resources and realized that women cannot rely solely on their beauty to succeed. She went on to become the first woman prime minister of Israel, and at the age of seventy-one, and was characterized as a paragon of dedication, a mover of mountains.

Emme Aronson, who is five feet eleven and weighs 190 pounds, is the leading model for sizes fourteen and above. Many women would give their eyeteeth to have her looks. She maintains that it's all a matter of attitude. She admits that she will never be a size ten again, but she still feels great and she doesn't have to cover her body with a towel.

People who possess attitudes of insecurity and inferiority are usually uncertain about doing things correctly, so they seek and need approval. They consider others better because of their talents, training, and treasure. In so many instances, ninety-nine positive strokes that they have received are erased by one negative stroke.

In a *Peanuts* comic strip, Charlie Brown is asked, "What's that you're wearing around your neck?"

Charlie answers, "It's a medical tag…lots of people wear them."

The questioner continues by asking, "What does it say?"

Charlie responds, "Insecure."

Many of us identify with this clumsy, inadequate human being and that undoubtedly explains his popularity.

Another enemy of a good attitude is resentment. Resentful people will blame God, their boss, others, or any available scapegoat. They go through life with a chip on their shoulders and act like the older son in the prodigal son story. They become bitter people rather than better people. Their fists double up as their fingernails cut deeply into their own hands because of some injury done to them. Instead of becoming wounded healers, they wound others. They easily fall into the quicksand of self-pity and develop a search-and-destroy attitude.

Saul became very resentful of David because "Saul has killed his thousands, and David his ten thousands" (1 Sam 18:7). Saul's one ambition was to kill David. His search-and-destroy attitude ended by him falling on his own sword. Resentful people inflict more harm on themselves than they do on others.

According to Chapter Six in Mark's Gospel, Jesus could not perform his mighty works in the country where he grew up. How could an ordinary carpenter do such works? It was because of his countrymen's attitude, their biases and preconceptions, that he did not heal much in their territory. Jesus said, "Prophets are not without honor, except in their hometown, and among their own kin, and in their own house" (Mark 6:4).

Christians with negative attitudes have a very narrow vision of life. That was certainly true of the scribes and Pharisees. Saint Peter had to broaden his horizons, especially regarding the religious practices of circumcision and what foods were considered clean and unclean. Minds once stretched cannot return to their original shape. The only way parachutes work is when they are open.

We often suffer some of the same biases or prejudices. Some Christians inflict much pain on single women. Alice Mathews, a professor of Educational Ministries and Women's Ministries, states, "They are not considered 'adults' until they are married. They are called 'girls' until they wed, not withstanding their professional achievement or their spiritual maturity. Single women sense others' assumption that being married is the only 'right' and 'godly' goal they should have. This, of course, flies in the face of the apostle Paul's teaching in I Corinthians 7 as well as the example of his own life."[3]

A family doctor, psychologist, or psychiatrist can help us to the extent we cooperate with him or her. Psychotherapists point out how the patient's attitude is of utmost importance to the progress of the therapy. I remember a friend of mine telling me how he didn't get much help from a psychologist he was visiting. I am convinced it was because of his negative attitude toward the psychologist.

Positive Attitudes

We need to be aware of these and many other negative attitudes. They are like sand traps or the water hazards on a golf course. A good golfer avoids them and tries to put the ball on the green. To accomplish that goal, we need to develop positive attitudes.

A positive attitude is better than drugs or alcohol. We often make the mistake of thinking that the approach needed is a matter of talent or aptitude. I know a number of people who have a lot of talent or aptitude, but their attitude leaves much to be desired. As the saying goes, it is not aptitude but attitude that will determine our altitude in life.

There are balcony people and basement people. Basement people usually have negative attitudes because they don't want to see too much. Balcony people have positive attitudes and thereby see what needs to be done. Dwight Eisenhower insisted that without a positive attitude toward the commander of the troops, victory was impossible.

By saying yes to life and all it offers Christians develop a positive attitude. Saint Paul speaks of Jesus as "not 'Yes' and 'No' but in him it is always 'Yes'" (2 Cor 1:19). Life *is* very exciting; it is only dull and boring to dull and boring people. Before we can do something, as Goethe said, we have to be something. Jesus spent only three years preaching, teaching, and healing. He treated every person with whom he came in contact as the most important person.

People want to feel respected and loved. We need a collaborative attitude that implies respect for others' opinions and feelings, active listening—not planning what we are going to say next. This process is as important as the product. Billy Graham is not known as a very glib speaker or a bible scholar, but he is dedicated to meeting other people's needs and concerns and not his own.

Russian novelist Aleksandr Solzhenitsyn said of the West that the time to save itself is gone. The only way it can is to change its attitudes. We have too many cranky, cantankerous people who have become dried up. Many of them have become CCC people—Constant Chronic Complainers. They are never satisfied and continually find fault with everyone and everything. They can be recognized by their narrowness of mind. Truth is no longer accessible to them. Their reality has become very small, practically keyhole size.

Jesus met these individuals when he was about to heal the man with the withered hand. He asked the Pharisees, "Is it lawful to do or harm on the Sabbath, to save life or to kill it?" Saint Mark tells us that "they were silent. He looked around at them with anger; he was grieved at their hardness of heart" (Mark 3:4–5).

This was a justified anger because they refused to even consider the possibility of tampering with the Sabbath. Structures, rules, and laws often will not change people, but positive attitudes will. Many of us close our minds, like rusty bear traps, to the possibility of change in our lives. Our minds have become fixed, our attitudes locked into an irreversible position.

What is needed is Jesus' redemption from fixation. Jesus' attitude toward sinners, tax collectors, prostitutes, and lepers was difficult for the scribes and Pharisees to accept. Tax collectors, prostitutes and lepers were considered outcasts or culturally taboo. Jesus was not afraid to touch lepers, which made a person legally unclean. He asked Zacchaeus to dine with him. To share a table with someone meant to share his or her life, a guarantee of trust, peace, and friendship. "All who saw it began to grumble and said, 'He has gone to be the guest of one who is a sinner'" (Luke 19:7). They refused to change their attitude.

A positive attitude will enable us to handle and prevent unnecessary stress more effectively. Stressful feelings will cloud positive attitudes and cause us to view life more pessimistically. Stressful people usually expect the worst, look at the dark side of things, and don't expect things to go their way. Christians with a positive attitude expect the best, look at the bright side of things, and expect things to go their way. They also are joy-filled people. Religion is *supposed* to help us be joyful, but some Christians have just enough religion to make them miserable. When we are intent on being rather than having or possessing, we will be more joyful and not rob others of being who they are. Joy for the saints was only as deep as their pain. That helps explain how they could be so joyful despite suffering so much. They kept dancing on wounded legs.

G. K. Chesterton maintained that joy is a Christian's secret but many have rather sad faces, looking as if they are following a hearse through life or have been baptized in lemon juice. Father John Catoir, former director of the Christophers, writes that if there is joy in our hearts, we should notify our faces. "A glad heart makes a cheerful countenance" (Prov 15:13). Someone has said that as we grow older we receive the face we deserve. Dorothy Day called joy a "duty of delight."

Joy when separated as three individual letters can symbolize:

J for Jesus
O for others
Y for yourself

That is the order of our priorities: we put Jesus first, others second, and ourselves last. Then we will not so easily indulge in self-pity. When I come across someone who does this, I recommend that they visit someone in a nursing home, a hospital, or a hospice.

Leon Bloy maintained that joy is a definite sign of the Holy Spirit's presence. Jesus prayed at the Last Supper "that my joy may be in you, and that your joy may be complete" (John 15:11). True joy is always rooted in God's love and God's love never changes. Pleasures will fade but joy will always abide. God created us to be happy with him forever in heaven. Mirth comes from God, dullness from the devil.

Pope Benedict XVI in *Deus Caritas Est* (no. 3) states that joy is God's gift to us and a foretaste of the Divine. Paul's joy never faded. Even when in prison, he wrote, "Rejoice in the Lord always; again I will say, Rejoice" (Phil 4:4). The real challenge for Christians is to rejoice when they are suffering or in pain. Saint James wrote, "Whenever you face trials of any kind, consider it nothing but joy" (Jas 1:2). The psalmist tells us, "May those who sow in tears reap with shouts of joy" (Ps 126:5). "A cheerful heart is a good medicine, but a downcast spirit dries up the bones" (Prov 17:22). One of the best things we need up our sleeves is a funny bone. Joy is a running stream, not stagnant water. Christians with joy-filled hearts are known for their positive attitudes and for reaching out to others.

Change of Attitude Needed

Only people with a passion for what is possible are open to change, especially a change of attitude. Truth is accessible for them because they are always pursuing it. Their reality becomes broader, like a prism revealing new angles and understandings. They are searching like Nicodemus, who came to Jesus at night and wanted to know more about being reborn. Or the Ethiopian eunuch who replied to Philip's question of whether he grasped what he was reading: "How can I, unless someone guides me?" (Acts 8:30–31).

We often cannot change some situations, but we can always change our attitude. We have to concentrate more on our advantages rather than our disadvantages, on what we have rather than what we don't have. The light at the end of the tunnel is not the headlight of an oncoming train. Face life with all its harsh realities, not as we think it is or wish it were. Squeeze all the enjoyment we can out of life. Too many of us settle for mediocrity or a dull and boring existence. Life is exciting and adventurous to people with positive attitudes. They are anxious and look forward to the next challenge.

Our attitude will often manifest itself when we drive. Experts point out that our attitude is the car's most important safety feature. Dr. Francis Kenel, a traffic safety consultant, found that those drivers who showed the extremes of overcontrol or undercontrol had terrible driving records. Their attitudes became very evident as they drove their cars. Many of us have witnessed this when we are passengers in their cars.

When baby-boomer Catholics were asked in a survey if they could be a good Catholic without going to mass every Sunday, 77 percent of males and 90 percent of females answered yes. When also asked if they could be a good Catholic not obeying the church's opposition to abortion, 67 percent of males and 69 percent of females replied positively. Do these attitudes indicate a secular influence of our American culture where personal opinion is held in high regard?[4]

Researchers have found that our attitude ultimately determines whether we possess a challenge or a choke response. In a challenge response, we rise to the occasion and meet it, whereas a choke response ends in failure because of the inability to perform under stress. Athletes are often accused of a choke response when they are unable to perform under stressful moments. Then they often have recourse to violence.

Mike Singletary, a former linebacker for the Chicago Bears, boldly stated that a good attitude leads to greatness. He was able to overcome his physical shortcomings through dedication and persistence. Singletary became a man obsessed, and he readily admitted it.

It is a proven fact that people with good attitudes gravitate to the top. Joe Paterno, in his autobiography, tells how reading Virgil's *Aeneas* shaped his attitudes, especially toward success and competition. He turned down an offer of $1.4 million dollars to become the coach and general manager of the New England Patriots and stayed as coach with Penn State. Tom Brokaw has said that it's much easier to make a dollar and much harder to make a difference. Christians with positive attitudes make a difference.

Jesus made a difference by his attitude. Some of his most scathing remarks were made against the scribes and Pharisees because they had such negative attitudes. They were legalists and observed every iota of the law except the most important one to love God, others, and themselves. Jesus produced such positive results because of his positive attitudes. What we receive from what we do is equal to our attitude when we do it. A negative attitude will work against us, whereas a positive attitude will work for us. A positive attitude looks for ways to solve problems, not create them. It provides us the opportunity to let go of things over which we have no control.

I remember visiting a homebound person in one of the suburbs of Detroit. She had rheumatoid arthritis in her hands that prevented her from even holding a telephone. In the course of our conversation, she said to me, "You know, Father, I thank God each day for my suffering." Needless to say, I was overwhelmed by her statement. To arrive at this juncture in one's life is a special grace and a positive attitude. We so easily complain when things don't go our way or we lose control of a situation. It is not easy to say, "Thank you, God" when we can't get our car started or burn the toast. We don't realize how much we want to be in control of our lives, the lives of others, and even God.

We make choices every day regarding what our attitude will be. In many instances we cannot change the people we deal with, but we can always change ourselves, especially our attitude. As the popular maxim states, "life is 10 percent of what happens to us and 90 percent how we react to it." A positive attitude will also help develop healthy expectations. A healthy expectation is "This is what I would like or hope for, but I won't be disappointed if it does not happen." Unhealthy expectations are often expressed as demands: "I should or must get..."

Saint Paul expressed it so well when he wrote that your attitude must be that of Christ, "Who though he was in the form of God, did not regard equality with God as something to be exploited, but emptied himself, taking the form of a slave, being born in human likeness. And being found in human form, he humbled himself and became obedient to the point of death— even death on a cross" (Phil 2:6–8). One of Christianity's greatest paradoxes is our ability to lose our life to save it. Like Jesus, in the dying process, we find life, life eternal.

If we want to develop positive attitudes, Jesus can teach us how. He did not let the negative attitude of the scribes and Pharisees affect him. He realized life is too short to give in to negative attitudes. He tried to change other people's attitudes and found much resistance. His attitude toward sinners and outcasts challenges us to examine our own prejudices and biases. His belief that every person is important and needs respect was demonstrated with the adulteress, the woman at the well, and Mary Magdalene. His positive attitude toward who he was and his mission allowed him to go up to Jerusalem to suffer, die, and rise that we might have new life. Our challenge as Christians is to be able to share his life and positive attitude with others.

SCRIPTURE PASSAGES FOR REFLECTION

"A glad heart makes a cheerful countenance." (Prov 15:13)

"Prophets are not without honor, except in their hometown, and among their own kin, and in their own house." (Mark 6:4)

"Do all things without murmuring or arguing." (Phil 2:14)

"I know your works; you are neither cold nor hot." (Rev 3:15)

QUESTIONS TO CONSIDER

1. What kind of attitude do we reflect?

2. Do we have any negative attitudes toward others or ourselves?

3. What positive attitudes do we manifest?

4. Do we consider ourselves joy-filled people?

5. Do we find it difficult to change an attitude?

9

CONFLICTING OPINIONS ON WEALTH

"It is easier for a camel to go through the eye of a needle than for someone who is rich to enter the kingdom of God."
Mark 10:25

Despite having a positive attitude toward others and all of life, there still will be conflicts facing any Christian. One of the conflicts is wealth. Wealth is indeed a difficult challenge for all of us, especially because the Bible presents conflicting opinions on it.

Wealth is often portrayed in the Bible as good. God promises prosperity to those who are faithful, yet the rich are derided for their greed and exploitation. Wisdom literature presents us with the best outlook on wealth:

"Riches and honor are with me, enduring wealth and prosperity." (Prov 8:18)
"If riches are a desirable possession in life, what is richer than wisdom, the active cause of all things?" (Wis 8:5)
"Riches are good if they are free from sin; poverty is evil only in the opinion of the ungodly." (Sir 13:24)
Jabez prayed to God, "Oh that you would bless me and enlarge my border, and that your hand might be with me,

and that you would keep me from hurt and harm! And God granted what he asked." (1 Chr 4:10)

Wealth or money in First-World countries is far more challenging than sex or politics. Wealth implies power, privilege, status, being an insider, climbing the ladder of success, and having a corner on all the resources like food, water, and oil. Wealth has many shades of meaning. We often speak of a "wealth of information or knowledge," which is another way of looking at wealth. In one of her shows, Oprah Winfrey said that as a child she thought that all white people were rich or wealthy.

Jesus makes it clear that wealth often prevents us from knowing and being part of the reign of God. Jesus spoke more about wealth than he did about prayer. He had rich friends like Nicodemus and Joseph of Arimathea. Nicodemus brought the myrrh and aloes to anoint his body (John 19:38–39). Some women of means ministered to him during his public ministry (Mark 15:40–41). He certainly visited the home of Martha and Mary often (Luke 10:38). Zacchaeus was certainly rich, but Jesus dined with him (Luke19:5). What Jesus preached against was exploiting the poor and greed in its various forms.

Affluence or wealth in itself is not sinful but is God's gift as is brought out in Wisdom literature. When it becomes, however, a Christian's pursuit or enjoyment and results in making us callous to other's sufferings or needs, there is injustice. Economic advancement can cause poverty for others. How often we hear of a work plant relocating and leaving in its wake hundreds of unemployed. An expanding economy, which has many benefits, often widens the gap between the rich and poor. Doesn't our market economy favor the rich and exploit the poor? Doesn't the world thrive on a lower economic class? The rich and wealthy become richer and the poor become a blip on the screen.

According to a recent survey, "the top one percent of Americans rose 157 percent at the same time that the lowest 20 percent of wage earners actually lost ground in earnings."[1] Another way of stating this is that the wealthiest 20 percent of our world's population gets almost 83 percent of our world's income while the poorest 20 percent get less than 2 percent. The average chief executive officer receives $1,566 an hour while the average worker receives $7.39.[2]

"World Resources Institute says that someone living in a developed nation uses twice as much grain, three times as much meat, nine times as much paper, and eleven times as much gasoline as someone living in a developing nation. The problem is not a lack of resources but the way those resources are being disproportionately consumed. Another window into the same reality: 16 percent of the world's population spends 80 percent of the world's private consumption."[3] Five hundred of the richest persons in the world own and control resources available to 460 million of the poor.

Many of us have seen the statistics concerning the Global Village that is a challenge to any Christian. Imagine shrinking the earth into a village of one hundred people. The results are: fifty-seven Asians, twenty-one Europeans, fourteen from the Western Hemisphere, and eight Africans. Fifty-two people would be female and forty-eight male. Seventy people would be nonwhite and thirty would be white. Seventy people would be non-Christian and thirty would be Christian. Eighty-nine people would be heterosexual and eleven homosexual. Six individuals would possess 59 percent of the entire world's wealth (all six would be Americans). Eighty people would live in substandard housing. Seventy people would be unable to read. Fifty individuals would suffer from malnutrition. One would be near death and one would be near birth. One would have a college education, and one own a computer.[4] Those are sobering statistics especially for Christians. We might spend some time thinking about and reflecting upon them.

We live in a global world now webbed through transportation and communication. One can fly from Chicago to New Delhi in eleven hours. The computer has linked us instantaneously to far-away countries even the most remote locations. We are also a global planet whose population is getting younger. It is estimated that the majority of those on the global planet by 2010 will be under eighteen years of age. Most of us, because of the birthing cycle, will be in the minority. One of the most critical aspects of our Christian growth in a global world is to know who we are and how we relate. We are not the center of the universe but only a part of it. Our task as Christians is to help others see the sacred in what is fragmented and even sinful, promoting a life-giving lifestyle.

Bono, the famous singer and entertainer, is someone who understands this challenge. He suggested at the 2006 National Prayer Breakfast that one percent of our federal budget be tithed to the poor. Then a girl in Africa will be able to go to school, an AIDS patient will get her or his medicine. It could transform millions of lives. According to a recent report, the median wealth for African Americans is ten times less than whites. Unemployment remains twice as high for blacks than whites. African Americans have more difficulties getting loans and mortgages. They are still being barred from buying homes in certain neighborhoods.

African Americans, whose homes were destroyed by urban development, have suffered from what Mindy Thompson Fullilove, a research psychiatrist, calls root shock, which is a stressful reaction to a tragic situation affecting all or part of a person's emotional ecosystem. It is comparable to a painful traffic accident where the body fluids are lost cutting off circulation to arms and legs. If the fluids are not quickly restored, a person can die. Root shock has also happened to people who have suddenly lost their homes and possessions due to a hurricane like Katrina, a tornado, or some other natural disaster.

As Christians we need to respond to these situations and not remain paralyzed. Only when our paralyzed hearts are healed can we get up and walk. Too often we are good, silent witnesses to our faith, but we need to reach out to touch someone. In Milwaukee, Wisconsin, Project Ripple Effect has been initiated for people to do just that. It is designed to gather together average folks and projects in need. The founders believed that spending an hour a week helping some worthy cause will result in a ripple effect in the community. Other cities have expressed interest and want to set up similar programs. Certainly, Christians could spare an hour a week.

Money

Is money the root of all kinds of evil? (cf. 1 Tim 6:10). Not in all instances, especially when money is looked upon as a tool for good or evil.

As Christians, it is far easier to look upon money as the demon corrupting those who have so much. Christians have increased their income over the last thirty years, but it has been proven that the richer we become the less we give. If Christians tithed, we would have $143 billion available to help the poor and help to "spread the Good News." If we believe that God is very concerned with the poor, how do we explain the contradiction between belief and practice?[5] Has our love become too shallow or limited, or are we becoming more vindictive? We side more with what divides us than what unites us, we and they, rather than we. We need a win/win strategy that will save our nation and planet.

If money is the root of all evil, consumerism and materialism rank close to it. "The lover of money will not be satisfied with money; nor the lover of wealth, with gain. This also is vanity"

(Eccl 5:9). "Give me neither poverty nor riches; feed me with the food I need" (Prov 30:8). Amos hammered away at the injustices of the rich, "For I know how many are your transgressions, and how great are your sins" (Amos 5:12). Because he spoke so forcefully against the foolishness of power and riches, he was called the prophet of social justice.

Jesus, the greatest prophet, made it very clear that "It is easier for a camel to go through the eye of a needle than for someone who is rich to enter the kingdom of God" (Mark 10:25). Jesus pulled the apostles through the needle's eye and introduced them to the simplicity and freedom of the kingdom. How do we challenge ourselves to live in solidarity with the poor? Many teachers, doctors, dentists, nurses, and others go to Third World countries and freely give of their time, talent, and treasure to alleviate the poor and their situation. My doctor goes every year. Some attorneys give their services pro bono. Indeed, this outreach is most inspirational and life-giving.

One form of power, however, is money. Money is power and prestige. As many rich people find out, however, money is not the answer to happiness. Just ask people who have won a lottery, or others who have inherited or made a lot of money. Some of the poorest people I have met and know are some of the happiest people. Howard Hughes was asked, "With all your money, are you happy?" He replied, "No." According to marriage experts, spouses argue most over money matters, causing much strife and unhappiness.

Craving after money can become a god in some people's lives. What are our self-made gods? Our god can be any value to which we give highest place in our lives. This will often be revealed to us in times of searing struggles or when choosing between two values. This value can be work, health, money, overeating, drink, drugs, immoral sex, or anything that controls us. Jesus put it succinctly, "For where your treasure is, there your heart will be also" (Matt 6:21).

What do we think of or want most? Where are our thoughts centered? There is our hearts. We need to remind ourselves to "Keep your lives free from the love of money, and be content with what you have" (Heb 13:5). We need to stress more what we have rather than what we don't have. When Dorothy Day was asked to comment on Jesus' words, "Give therefore to the emperor the things that are the emperors, and to God the things that are God's" (Matt 22:21), she replied that if people rendered to God what belongs to God, Caesar would have nothing left. If the coin presented to Jesus bears the emperor's image, then we need to ask what bears God's image?

When seen in the light of the Genesis, in which God says let us make humankind in our image, the answer is obvious, the human person. That is our challenge as Christians: to image God's love, goodness, and justice. Pope Benedict XVI in his encyclical *Deus Caritas Est* states "The two spheres (Church and state) are distinct, yet always interrelated" (no. 28).

One way to image God's love and justice is to simplify our lifestyle by not relentlessly pursuing more money. For some that might mean a major overhaul of their lives, and for others a tune up. Part of the equation is to determine how much money is enough. We can also simplify our lives by watching less television, getting rid of clutter, slowing down, reducing one's debt, not buying clothes that need to be dry-cleaned, and getting rid of all but one or two credit cards, just to mention a few ways. However, many of us have embraced a frenetic lifestyle of becoming workaholics. Increased salary means more time spent away from family. So is the American way of life, as Ari Fleischer, the former press secretary for President George W. Bush, once proclaimed, "a blessed one"?

Greed

Greed has been defined in various ways, but some consider it a soul sickness. No wonder the prophets lashed out against it, and the fathers of the church named it one of the deadly sins.

Most of us are guilty of this vice because as Americans we consume more of the world's resources than needed. So it is a social vice. We need to ask why we are greedy. One reason is our reluctance to share. We can be greedy not only for money or material things, but also for prestige, power and success. We want more, and in this process shut others out thereby hurting ourselves as well as the community. Increased power often results in less concern and attention given to others.

A powerful example of greed can be found in Gollum in the *Lord of the Rings*. He dies trying to regain the ring. Recent corporate scandals are other examples of greed, demonstrating how top executives unjustly take the company's assets, depriving employees of their pensions and jobs. It is easy to notice how others are greedy, wanting more, and those who are in the denial stage. As Christians we need to be true, however, to the gospel. I have not come across too many people who have prayed for less. We need to imitate John the Baptist who said, "Whoever has two coats must share with anyone who has none; and whoever has food must do likewise" (Luke 3:11).

Mother Teresa explained the problem in this way, "The trouble is that rich people, well-to-do people, very often don't really know who the poor are; and that is why we can forgive them, for knowledge can only lead to love, and love to service. And so if they are not touched by them, it's because they do not know them."[6] Her demeanor has been described as meek, but when it came to the poor she was like a pit bull, not letting go.

Jesus counseled the official who asked, "Good Teacher, what must I do to inherit eternal life?" Besides observing the commandments, he said, "There is still one thing lacking. Sell all that you own and distribute the money to the poor, and you will have treasure in heaven. Then come, follow me" (Luke 18:18–22). He could not respond to this invitation, and this is one of the saddest stories in the gospel. How many Christians would be able to respond to this invitation from Jesus? Zacchaeus, once he encountered Jesus said, "Look, half of my possessions, Lord, I will give to the poor; and if I have defrauded anyone of anything, I will pay back four times as much" (Luke 19:8). Sons and daughters of Abraham do this. Do we?

Jesus could have told the official to renounce all that he had, but he tells him to go one step further, to give the proceeds to the poor. Jesus embraces the biblical concern for the poor as brought out in the Hebrew Scriptures. He also invites all of us into his ministry of sharing the good news especially with the poor. However, we would rather live with people who are like us. We become nervous and suspicious with people who are different. Recall how someone said to Jesus, "Teacher, tell my brother to divide the family inheritance with me." He replied, "Friend, who set me to be a judge or arbitrator over you?" Then he said to the crowd, "Take care! Be on your guard against all kinds of greed; for one's life does not consist in the abundance of possessions" (Luke 12:13–15). Jesus also said, "But when you give alms, do not let your left hand know what your right is doing, so that your alms may be done in secret; and your Father who sees in secret will reward you" (Matt 6:3–4). Anonymous donors are truly to be commended. Jesus and his apostles were taken care of by women like Mary Magdalene; Joanna, the wife of Herod's steward Chuza; Susanna; and many others who provided for them out of their resources. They were willing to share themselves as so many women in the church do today. Where would the church be today without so many dedicated women?

We read in the Acts of the Apostles, "Now the whole group of those who believed were of one heart and soul...There was not a needy person among them, for as many as owned lands or houses sold them and brought the proceeds of what was sold. They laid it at the Apostles' feet and it was distributed to each as any had need" (Acts 4:32–35). This characterized the early community as depicted by Luke. It follows that if they were of one mind and heart they would share their possessions and give them to the apostles.

Contrast this with what follows. Ananias and Sapphira hoarded their possessions and lied about the amount; this action resulted in their deaths. A teacher was telling this story to a group of small children. At the end, one of the children raised his hand and said, "If God did that today, there would not be too many people around!" How true! The movie *Brokeback Mountain* is a powerful example of how destructive dishonesty with others and oneself can be, and the consequences of leading a double life. Later in the Acts of the Apostles, we read how deacons were elected to take care of the widows who were being neglected (Acts 6:1). Saint Paul quotes the words of Jesus, "It is more blessed to give than to receive" (Acts 20:35). Do we live like that?

Will There Be Enough?

Global questions need to be addressed by Christians: Will there be enough housing, food, clothing, and medical and educational care to meet all people's needs, especially with so much poverty and suffering running rampant? Personal questions to consider might be: Will I have enough of a pension fund, especially when these funds have declined by one-third of their value? Will I be able to retire at sixty-five with our teetering economy or will I have to go back to work as many have once they retired? If there isn't enough to go around, some will have to do without. Eight hundred and fifty million people suffer from malnourishment and food insecurity; witness the starving child in Latin America who came into church at communion time and asked, "Is there any left for me?" We have the agricultural and technical ability to end hunger, but we are caught up in the paralysis of analysis instead of action. In our hungers, we need to feed the hungry; in our brokenness and bruises we need to become wounded healers; in our anxiety and fear we need to comfort the afflicted.

We read in Luke's Gospel how Jesus was in a deserted place and crowds swelled to hear him. He spoke to them about the reign of God and healed those in need. Because the day was drawing to a close, he told the disciples to dismiss the crowds and give them something to eat. They replied, "We have not more than five loaves and two fish—unless we are to go and buy food for all these people." So Jesus instructed them to have the five thousand recline in groups of fifty. "And taking the five loaves and the two fish, he looked up to heaven, and blessed and broke them, and gave them to the disciples to set before the crowd. And they ate and were filled, What was left over was gathered up, twelve baskets of broken pieces" (Luke 9:11–17). Another interpretation to this story is that some people brought food along and were then asked to share it with others who did not bring any food. The assumption here is that God will provide what we need. God's creation implies that there will be enough for birds, fish, animals, and human beings, but that means equal distribution. Are we ready to accept and act on this challenge?

Wants and Needs

Christians need to be more aware of the difference between wants and needs. Certainly not everything that we want is what we need. We are constantly bombarded by means of television, radio, newspapers, and magazines, to buy, buy, and, of course, pay later. We all know the saying, "Shop until you drop."

Naturally we want more things, but do we really need them? A ripple effect results when those in the First World get what they want but people in the Third World don't get what they need. It is also true that when the government gives the richest people tax cuts, it reduces benefits and services for the poor. How guilty are we as a church in identifying with the upper class or a higher social level? Plato once said that simplicity does not mean we have to live in misery and poverty. What it means is we have what we need, and we do not want anything we do not need.

Excessive wealth not shared can be a cancer to many. It was certainly true of Solomon, wise as he was. How do we explain escalating levels of homelessness and hunger in the richest country in the world? Saint Ambrose maintained that nature doesn't make distinctions between rich and poor but treats all the same. He asks if there is any difference between one dead man and another. You've never seen a U-haul behind a hearse. One pastor insisted, "You can't take the money with you, but you can always send it ahead." How do we explain that many have financial resources, a nice home, health care, and additional social amenities, while others live in dire poverty?

One of the main reasons for the discrepancy is that many in this country are born into a white, middle-class culture and have opportunities that don't exist elsewhere. Millions of people in the United States are still without adequate income. The majority of people who become poor do so because of a loss of a job or a family breakup. Therefore, the war on poverty needs to be fought on two fronts: employment opportunities and family stability. God does not desire poverty but expects people to be accountable for how they treat the poor. The poor, not the rich, tell us what is right or wrong. According to Walter Brueggemann, an Old Testament scholar, God is preoccupied with the poor. Giving is meant not only to relieve suffering but also to eliminate it. Virtue or desire alone never feeds the poor and hungry. Giving matters as much as how we give. Saint James admonishes us, "Be doers of the word and not merely hearers who deceive themselves" (Jas 1:22).

Christians need to ask if they share or hoard what they have. We need to ask questions about the wise and foolish virgins (cf. Matt 25:1–13). Did the wise ones point out ahead of time that the others would not have enough oil? Were they really afraid they would not have enough if they shared their oil? Did they really enjoy themselves once they entered the banquet hall? Did Jesus spend time trying to answer these questions? Knowing the plight of others, how can we enjoy our many blessings if we don't share them? How can we enjoy health care when millions of people don't have it, or food when others are starving?

Oliver Bennett, who teaches at Warwick University, contends in *Cultural Pessimism: Narratives of Decline in the Postmodern World* that even though Western countries have become more wealthy, many are suffering from deep depression. Why? Because of the increase of terrorism, drugs, AIDS, gang warfare, and the inequality between rich and poor. The belief is that we can't make a better world. We live between the Big Bang and the Big Chill.

However, our Christian hope does offer something to our parched world. In our thirst to help others, do we find ourselves drawing water from the wrong well? Despite the crises of hopelessness, we believe that ultimately good will triumph over evil, that suffering and death will end. Julian of Norwich, like Saint Paul, was convinced that evil increased so that grace might more abound. She maintained that evil's stranglehold on the world would not triumph. We have our Good Friday but it is followed by Easter and a risen Christ who is our hope as the Emmaus disciples said, "But we had hope that he was the one to redeem Israel" (Luke 24:21).

We don't lose hope despite the crisis surrounding us. The church was born in crisis and was rejuvenated. The same can happen now if we are a hope-filled people. The church did not collapse during the fourth century when most of the bishops were Arian. Jesus gave us a gilt-edge guarantee when he said to Peter, "You are Peter, and on this rock I will build my church, and the gates of Hades will not prevail against it" (Matt 16:18).

Words Known by the Company They Keep

If the saying is true that words are known by the company they keep, we need to look at Mary's Magnificat: the proud are contrasted with the humble and the rich with the hungry (cf. Luke 1:51–53). We see this truth in Jesus' parable of the rich man and Lazarus (cf. Luke 16:19–31). What a hyperbolic contrast between how these two men are clothed and the lavish banquet table where one eats abundantly and Lazarus receives a few crumbs. We often overlook the rich man's compassion when he implored Abraham, "I beg you to send him to my father's house—for I have five brothers—that he may warn them, so that they too will not also come into the place of torment." But his compassion is misplaced because it focuses on the inner circle, his brothers. That is the concern of the rich and wealthy, their friends or rich people, so they are able to be repaid. Then Jesus makes it clear that they have their reward. He also declared that when having a banquet to "invite the poor, the crippled, the lame, the blind; blessed indeed will you be because of their inability to repay you. For you will be repaid at the resurrection of the righteous" (Luke 14:13–14). How many Christians feast at the banquet table while Lazarus lies out in the street begging for some crumbs?

Albert Schweitzer, when reflecting on this parable, was inspired to become a doctor and went to Africa to relieve the ills of thousands. Contrast Jesus' Sermon on the Mount in the fifth chapter of Matthew's Gospel, "Blessed are you who are poor, for yours is the kingdom of God," to "But woe to you who are rich, for you have received your consolation" (Luke 6:24). Jesus certainly viewed the world through a different set of lenses as he proclaimed the Beatitudes. They really are the *Magna Carta* of Christianity. If we want to find out what kind of Christians we are, pray them, and if anyone can say he or she fulfills them all, he or she certainly is a true disciple of Jesus.

Consider the parable of the rich man who wanted to tear down his barns and build larger ones so he could store more grain and other goods. Then he would be able to eat, drink, and be merry. He is considered a fool because his life will be demanded that very night (cf. Luke 12:16–21). How many are building huge homes with four private bathrooms, three fireplaces, a swimming pool, and a three-car garage? What would Jesus say to them?

Yes, riches and their proper use can be very challenging, but if we proclaim we are Christians, we cannot shun away from this responsibility. Jesus did not. He preached frequently about this subject because he knew human nature so well, our desire for power, privilege, status, and money, and always wanting more. We have to continue to remind ourselves to be attuned to the cry of the poor. We might not be able to end all the poverty, hunger, and pain, or resolve all the injustices, but all of us can share the responsibility of addressing it.

※ ※ ※

SCRIPTURE PASSAGES FOR REFLECTION

"Riches are good if they are free from sin; poverty is evil only in the opinion of the ungodly." (Sir 13:24)

"Give me neither poverty nor riches; feed me with the food I need." (Prov 3:8)

"There was not a needy person among them, for as many owned lands or houses sold them and brought the proceeds of what was sold. They laid it at the apostles' feet, and it was distributed to each as any had need." (Acts 4:34–35)

"It is more blessed to give than to receive." (Acts 20:35)

"Be doers of the word and not merely hearers who deceive themselves. (Jas 1:22)

QUESTIONS TO CONSIDER

1. How do the statistics concerning the Global Village challenge us?

2. Does craving after money become a god in our lives or cause much strife and unhappiness?

3. Where do we see the gap widening between rich and poor? What can be done about this?

4. How can we make sure there will be enough to meet other peoples' needs?

5. How can we be more aware of the distinction between what we want and what we really need?

10

OUTSIDERS VERSUS INSIDERS

Jesus said, *"For the least among all of you is the greatest."*
Luke 9:48

People who are wealthy certainly consider themselves or are considered "insiders" whereas the poor certainly consider themselves or are considered "outsiders." One of our strongest needs is to belong to a group, a community, or a family. This becomes evident because we are born into a family and belong to a certain culture.

African Americans, for example, seem to realize that to be human means belonging or being connected to a community. We begin to find our identity by our social and relational ties with others. However, in the process, different groups arise that are sometimes called insiders and outsiders, resulting in prejudices, discrimination, rivalries, and fear of strangers and foreigners. So the insiders flex their muscles to keep the outsiders out. If we are to live our Christian lives to the fullest, we need to address this problem.

The movie *The Outsiders* depicts a group of underprivileged teenagers who are attempting to belong to a family. They cannot find a family after their parents die and suffer abuse from their closest siblings and friends. So they join a gang known as the Greasers. The movie graphically depicts how we long to belong; otherwise, we end up as outsiders. Immigrants, for example, crave love and care. Korean-Americans often manifest this by sitting down every Sunday and sharing a meal together. They also share their trials and joys. This has become an important ritual for them.

The Bible shows how the people of Israel always felt that they were chosen by God among all the other peoples (cf. Gen 12:2–3). Actually, this was also a blessing for others. If that is true, the lines between outsider and insider diminish. Israel had to crush its enemies to survive, but they often forgot that they were chosen to proclaim God's goodness to others. This is evident from the words of Isaiah the prophet: "In the days to come, the mountain of the Lord's house shall be established as the highest of the mountains, and shall be raised above the hills; all the nations shall stream to it. Many peoples shall come and say, 'Come, let us go up to the mountain of the Lord, to the house of the God of Jacob; that he may teach us his ways and that we may walk in his paths" (Isa 2:2–3). A similar passage is found in Micah 4:1–2. These passages clearly show that all people are to come to the mountain and there worship God together. God's promise to Abram becomes a blessing for all people.

When people come together there are no outsiders; however, they will still remain Medes, Parthians, Elamites, inhabitants of Mesopotamia, Judea, and Cappadocia, Pontus and Asia (Acts 2:9–11). But the distinctions will not result in insiders and outsiders. Those marginalized will be part of the original group. Pentecost left no one on the sidelines. Is this true today?

Unity and division have been burning issues for many years. We long for unity and abhor division, especially the kind that isolates and fragments society. But we can pose the question, can there be legitimate and even scandalous divisions? The Tower of Babel and Pentecost are often used to point out the difference between unity and division. Luke's description of the tongues at Pentecost is in direct contrast to the tongues of Babel. In both situations, however, the people are confused. The one language spoken at Babel is disrupted and severed, while at Pentecost the many languages are understood by the listeners. People at Babel are dispersed and scattered, while unity and clarity are in evidence at Pentecost as the people are sent forth to preach reconciliation and love. In *Deus Caritas Est* Pope Benedict XVI states that it is the responsibility of the entire ecclesial community to practice love (no. 20).

The people at Babel are ego centered and want to make a name for themselves, while the people of Pentecost are "God centered." The people at Babel wanted to make a name for themselves that was not the name God gave Abram or Jacob, or Jesus gave to Peter. They wanted to impose a name on God so they would be socially significant. They were hoping to build a temple high enough so they could be assured of major favors from their god. We need to be aware how this concept continues to live on today. Conquering people may impose their language on those they defeat, hoping to unify them, when the opposite usually happens. Babylon did this. Today women and minorities are oppressed by language to conform to a certain culture. Some women are reduced to the physical appearance of their bodies to make them sex objects. Slaves were called slaves to demean them.

Walter Brueggemann maintains that even in the dispersal and scattering of people at Babel, God's plan of filling the earth was accomplished. In the Acts of the Apostles, Luke agrees with this insight. One of the purposes of his writing the Acts was to proclaim that salvation was extended to all gentiles. Luke has Saint Paul address this issue and global dispersion in his speech in

Athens (cf. Acts 17:24–27). Saint Paul makes it very clear that God cannot be captured in "shrines made by human hands" (Acts 17:24). People are dispersed so that they can find God again, but not for their own self-interests. Is this possible today?

Archbishop Desmond Tutu states, "Frequently when they attacked me for being involved in politics, I used to say, I wish I knew which Bible they were reading! Because the Bible I read was quite clear: God revealed God to the children of Israel, not in a sanctuary, but by carrying out a political act—freeing a bunch of slaves. Nothing could be more political. And yet it was also deeply religious. They then realized that the God who does this kind of thing must be a God who cares, who is biased in favor of the weak, the oppressed, the marginalized."[1] Walter Burghardt, SJ, the famous writer and preacher, states that "the preacher needs an eye and ear for the specific injustices to which the parishioners are subjected."[2]

Who Are the Outsiders?

Who are the outsiders? Hagar was definitely an outsider, especially to Sarah, who treated her shamefully (cf. Gen 16). However, God treats her like a human being; she is the first person in the Hebrew Scriptures encountered by an angel who promised her numerous descendants. She also is the only person who gives a name to God: "You are the God of seeing." Hagar is a symbol of how God shows love and care for all outsiders.

Outsiders might have a tendency to ask, "Why me, Lord?" rather than "Where are you, Lord?" Whose side is God on? God intervened for the Israelites when he delivered them from Pharaoh's oppression. God does not forget the poor or the cry of the afflicted (Ps 9:12). God sent Amos, condemning those "who oppress the poor, who crush the needy" (Amos 4:1). Dr. Martin Luther King Jr. quoted the prophet, "But let justice roll down like waters, and righteousness like an ever-flowing stream" (Amos 5:24). Isaiah pleaded with the people, "Learn to do good; seek justice, rescue the oppressed, defend the orphan, plead for the widow" (Isa 1:17). Pope Benedict XVI states in *Deus Caritas Est*: "Building a just and civil order, wherein each person receives what is his or her due, is an essential task which every generation must take up anew" (no. 28).

Whose side is God on? When God views the class struggles and distinctions, the racial conflicts and exploitations, God always takes the side of the oppressed and poor, the hopeless, the downtrodden, the outcasts of our society. According to some experts, the poorest of the poor are those in prison, especially those unjustly convicted. God has no partiality (Deut 10:17) and has a concern for the poor, as well as the rich. Pope Benedict XVI maintains that we need not make a distinction between rich and poor when showing love but need to reach out to widows, orphans, prisoners, and the sick and needy.

However, God will side with the poor, the despised, the afflicted, and the underdog when mistreated by the rich. God wants to reverse the contrast between the rich and the poor as found in Mary's Magnificat, "He has brought down the powerful from their thrones, and lifted up the lowly; he has filled the hungry with good things, and sent the rich away empty" (Luke 1:52–53). God doesn't demand that everyone have the same amount of possessions, money, or resources. What is to be avoided is that no one has an abundance at the expense of others with less. As it is written, "The one who had much did not have too much, and the one who had little did not have too little" (2 Cor 8:15).

Whose side is God on? Jesus said, "Blessed are the poor in spirit, for theirs is the kingdom of heaven" (Matt 5:3). The kingdom belongs to those who hunger, mourn, feel persecuted, and are excluded. Jesus says those who are last will be first: "For the least among all of you is the greatest" (Luke 9:48). God's kingdom belongs to all people. No one is left out. Carl Sandberg, a poet and historian, was once asked what he considered the ugliest word in the English language. After a long pause—and a longer pause—he exclaimed, *exclusion*. We need a web of inclusion, not exclusion.

Jesus and Outsiders

Jesus taught that outsiders are not excluded from God's caring activity. When the Roman centurion came to Jesus asking him to heal his servant, Jesus was amazed at his hope, love, and especially his faith. He was an outsider, but a man of whom Jesus could say that no one in all of Israel had such faith. Jesus went on to say, "Many will come from the east and the west and will eat with Abraham, and Isaac, and Jacob at the kingdom of heaven, while the heirs of the kingdom will be thrown into the outer darkness, where there will be weeping and gnashing of teeth" (Matt 8:10–12). This is a powerful example of how the insiders will be turned out and the outsiders invited in. Jesus himself was an outsider, more readily accepted by others than his own people. Is it any wonder that he could identify with them?

Another outsider was the Canaanite woman. Jews were instructed to stay away from the Canaanites because of their many sins and godlessness. She, like the Roman centurion, was not asking a favor for herself but for her daughter who was tormented by a demon. Jesus explores the tribal exclusions in his reply, "I was sent only to the lost sheep of the house of Israel. It is not fair to take the children's food and throw it to the dogs."

But she persisted by saying, "Even the dogs eat the crumbs that fall from their masters' table" (Matt 15:24–27). Her persistence and especially her faith were an indication she was ready to receive God's care for an outsider.

We Christians have to learn how to expand our hearts as Jesus did to the Roman centurion, the Canaanite woman, and many others. They were not beyond God's saving power, just like today's voiceless, weak, destitute, powerless, undocumented immigrants, and ghetto people. The best way to improve a slum or a ghetto is to put it out of existence, not just to displace it. We are called upon to help in this project.

The parable of the rich man and Lazarus, which was mentioned earlier, is another powerful example. Lazarus is an outsider covered with sores (licked by the dogs) who would have gladly taken the scraps spoken of by the Canaanite woman. However, the rich man in all his luxury fails to even give him that much. The gap between the two which the rich man could have closed grows even wider when he dies. Now it becomes an abyss or chasm. The roles are reversed and the rich man pleads with Abraham to have Lazarus "dip the tip of his finger in water and cool my tongue" (Luke 16:24). Abraham refuses because the rich man was supposed to have comforted or alleviated Lazarus while alive. Isn't this story being enacted today?

Saint John Chrysostom asked, "Do you want to honor Christ's body? Then do not scorn him in his nakedness, nor honor him here in Church with silken garments while neglecting him outside where he is cold and naked."[3] These are sober and challenging words for us.

Jesus attracted marginalized people while those who felt like the chosen ones kept their distance from them. To show his concern for the outcasts and the poor, Jesus used the image of a shepherd and his flock. Ezekiel used the same image of God (Ezek

34:11). As a good shepherd, Jesus went out after those who felt separated from the flock (John 10). Unlike Isaiah and Micah's vision, Jesus does not wait for them to come to him. He calls and they hear his voice. When they gather there will be one flock and one shepherd. When we receive the body and blood of Jesus, we say, "Amen." Do we believe we are becoming one with Christ, with the poor, the outcasts, with all who are at war or peace, with all who have different beliefs, with all who even hate us? In *Deus Caritas Est* Pope Benedict XVI notes the Eucharist is our opportunity to draw into Christ's most dynamic self-giving where we become one with others (nos. 13, 14).

Before Jesus ascended into heaven, he commissioned his disciples to carry on his work (cf. Matt 28:19). Outsiders no longer exist because all are invited to be insiders. Mary was present in the birth of the church at Pentecost. She who gave birth to her Son was included in the upper room when the birth of the church occurred with the coming of the Spirit: "All these were constantly devoting themselves to prayer, together with certain women, including Mary the mother of Jesus, as well as his brothers" (Acts 1:14). Saint Paul emphasizes "There is no longer Jew or Greek, there is no longer slave or free, there is no longer male and female, for all of you are one in Christ Jesus" (Gal 3:28). Naturally, gender, cultural, and social differences will always exist, but they are not to become a privilege. Greeks are equal to Jews, women to men, and there should be no social hierarchy because of position or status. Biased categories no longer exist, and, if they do, they must be broken down.

The world has winners and losers. The winners have advantages over losers because they get the breaks, succeed in obtaining their goals, keep climbing the ladder of success. Are we like Stephen R. Covey, a professor of business organization, who wanted to climb the social ladder only to find that he was up against the wrong wall? Losers often have the cards stacked against them and they end up at the bottom of the totem pole.

With whom do we Christians identify? Too often with the winners or insiders. The homeless certainly are outsiders or losers, and many of our streets have become dormitories for them. What can be done for them? It is possible for a disciplined person to become educated, or for a balanced diet to improve health, yet many people cannot overcome addictive habits or dysfunctional behavior. They often become the losers or outsiders and are in most need of our help. Too often we look the other way, expecting the government and social agencies to take care of these problems. Pope Benedict XVI claims that despite all our advances in science and technology, there is still much suffering and poverty in the world. Humanitarian efforts, he writes, need to continue to distribute food and clothing, provide housing and care for the poor. He referred to hunger as a scourge in his *Urbi et Orbi* address on Easter 2007.

On Mother's Day, some women can feel like outsiders or losers because they want to have children and cannot.[4] They often struggle with feelings of shame, guilt, and even fear that their spouse might leave them. One out of six couples, about six million, suffer from this ordeal. Adoption is an option, but that often is a long and painful process. Some couples doubt God's love and goodness. Some think a sin from the past has contributed to their infertility. Still others doubt that they would be good parents. We question why God allows bad things to happen to good people. Struggling with this dilemma is as baffling as trying to understand why Cho Seung Hui could kill thirty-two people at Virginia Tech University.

Single women can also consider themselves outsiders because they are some times forgotten or invisible in our society. Yet they play an important role in the church and society. Miriam,

Aaron's sister, was most likely single, and she was a leader of Israel (Mic 6:4). Saint Paul had a number of women who helped him: Phoebe, a minister of the church at Cenchreae (Rom 16:1), Mary (Rom16:6), and Tryphaena and Tryphosa (Rom 16:12).

We need to be aware of the plight of these individuals and not treat them as outsiders or losers. Covered with the grime and dust of September 11, 2001, we are all one color. The divisions between outsiders and insiders, rich and poor, homeless and home owners, married and single, mothers and infertile women, were eliminated. We became one—temporarily, just like people who flocked to churches after this traumatic event. Where are they now? What would those who died that day say to us now?

Are We Different?

Different is certainly not necessarily bad. I remember our rector in the minor seminary telling us that we have to "dare to be different." This did not mean we were encouraged to be odd balls. Christians are expected to be different in a good sense. Exclusion of others often blinds us to the biblical reality of God's care for all people. The bishops have made it clear that racism is a sin. Bill McCartney, founder of the Promise Keepers, maintains that one of the reasons for the drop off in attendance was their stand against racism.[5] We don't overcome racism by just talking to another race as was brought out by the conversation between radio talk-show host Don Imus and Rev. Al Sharpton Jr., about the controversy regarding comments that Imus had made about the Rutgers women basketball team in April 2007.

We overcome racism by integrating neighborhoods and addressing the deeper issues. The way we treat others might indicate how we treat God. Jesus made it clear that we are to broaden our guest list for a dinner. Why do we only invite certain people—for political purposes, to climb the ladder of success, or because others have invited us? How many of us are willing to invite the poor, the lame, the crippled, the blind, the person with HIV/AIDS, someone wearing a turban, an emotionally disabled child, a refugee, an immigrant, or even a prostitute—outsiders? These are the individuals who often experience discomfort, loneliness, insecurity, anxiety, and fear.

Hospitality involves an openness to new relationships, new possibilities for friendships, new people who might be different from us. Hospitality means that we don't label people as outsiders; we create a free, friendly, and safe environment for them. Hospitality is indeed a spiritual discipline but indispensable for us as Christians. It helps create kindred spirits and makes the lonely, insecure, anxious, and fearful feel wanted and appreciated.[6]

We are a nation earmarked with religious diversity, a staggering economy, racial prejudices, and social conflicts. Some social observers believe we are two Americas. When others don't agree with us or share our beliefs, they are labeled as different. Even the early Christian Church had to contend with whether the gentiles needed to be circumcised. Paul *care-fronted* Peter on this matter. Peter, as head of the church, was misguided and needed conversion, as many of us do. Peter finally realized that "If then God gave them the same gift that he gave us when we believed in the Lord Jesus Christ, who was I that I could hinder God?" (Acts 11:17). He realized that God was bigger, more inclusive, and more caring than he was. Those he considered outsiders God considered insiders.

Today we must consider church leaders, such as bishops, as well as state leaders who have feet of clay and might be misguided. As Christians we need to look for those who will lead and not mislead, for truth not half-truths or lies. Hope is found in integrity, not in inaccurate assumptions and conclusions that are not bolstered by true, factual data. We need to embrace values based on truth, fairness, integrity, respect, and love. Is our faith strong enough that it will never crash like a computer or need to be programmed? Jeremiah warned against putting our faith in a person: "Cursed are those who trust in mere mortals" (Jer 17:5). We need to put our complete trust in Jesus and we will never be disappointed. We will be disappointed, as many have, if we put our trust in others.

Saint Paul recognized the diversity of gifts given to all as a display of how the Spirit works (cf. 1 Cor 12:4–12). He also pointed out how we are to use those gifts: "prophecy, in proportion to faith; ministry, in ministering; the teacher, in teaching; the exhorter, in exhortation; the giver, in generosity; the leader, in diligence; the compassionate, in cheerfulness" (Rom 12:6–8). Once we put on or are clothed with Christ, we will better understand how all are gifted.

Dorothy Soelle states, "To attain the image of Christ means to live in revolt against the Pharaoh and to remain with the oppressed and disadvantaged. It means to make their lot one's own. It is easy to be on Pharaoh's side if one just blinks an eye. It is easy to overlook the crosses by which we are surrounded."[7]

In his book *Faith Beyond Resentment,* James Alison, a gay man, writes about his experience as an outsider. His perspective is certainly shared by many gay and lesbian people, as well as people of color. Women likewise are aware how men use them for their own purposes. Alison points out how outsiders become embittered and resentful. He compared himself to Jonah in the whale, but eventually felt Christ's love, which freed him. His message can help others in their struggle, especially to counteract the feelings of being an outsider. The question for us remains, how do we treat them?

It is difficult to relate to the stranger or outsider in our midst, not to oppress but to uplift them, not to shun but to welcome them, not to insult but to honor them, not to neglect but to protect them. Suffering and pain often lead to vengeance, hostility, bitterness, and resentment, rather than compassion, caring, and loving, which is how Jesus responded. The poor are often forgotten and neglected, but even worse is that they are not seen or are invisible. Yet, in *Deus Caritas Est,* Pope Benedict XVI uses the example of Saint Lawrence the martyr, who handed over to civil authorities the poor as the true treasures of the church.

Many African societies greet each other with "I see you." We need to find ways to see those invisible in our society, not seeing them as objects but as individuals deeply loved by God. The story is told by Murray Bodo, OFM, that when he was ready to fly to New Mexico, he told Dr. Karl Menninger how he dreaded to change planes at O'Hare airport. (I can identify with that.) Menninger told him that when he took his walk to his next connection, instead of dreading it, to make eye contact with as many people as possible, loving them with his eyes. Mother Teresa of Calcutta exhorted us to be God's kindness to others. In the slums be a light to the poor. To children and all who suffer from loneliness, lift them up with a smile. Give them your love and compassion, but especially your heart. How many of us have taken her words and put them into action?

❈ ❈ ❈

SCRIPTURE PASSAGES FOR REFLECTION

"Learn to do good; seek justice, rescue the oppressed, defend the orphan, plead for the widow." (Isa 1:17)

"He has brought down the powerful from their thrones, and lifted up the lowly." (Luke 1:52)

"If then God gave them the same gift that he gave us when we believed in the Lord Jesus Christ,who was I that could hinder God?" (Acts 11:17)

"There is no Jew or Greek, there is no longer slave or free, there is no longer male and female, for all of you are in Christ Jesus." (Gal 3:28)

QUESTIONS TO CONSIDER

1. Just as Saint Peter was misguided in his dealings with the early church, do we find the same is true of our leaders?

2. How is God reversing the rich and poor today, as found in Mary's Magnificat?

3. How is the story of the rich man and Lazarus reenacted today?

4. Who are the winners and losers in our society today?

5. How are the poor neglected, forgotten, and made invisible in our society?

11

WHO WILL SPEAK
FOR CHILDREN?

Jesus said, "Take care that you do not despise these little ones."
Matt 18:10

A pressing problem facing us is how we show greater concern for children. They are often treated as outsiders. Even in Jesus' time, children were thought to be least. Because an argument had arisen among the disciples about who is the greatest, Jesus said to them, "Whoever welcomes this child in my name welcomes me, and whoever welcomes me welcomes the one who sent me; for the least among all of you is the greatest" (Luke 9:48).

Welcoming God is an extraordinary idea because we often view God as welcoming us. This is indeed an often overlooked grace. By welcoming a child in God's name, we proclaim a gospel of reversal as is evident from Jesus' words. Jesus assured his listeners, "Truly I tell you, the tax collectors and the prostitutes are going into the kingdom of God ahead of you" (Matt 21:31). Jesus said to the twelve, "Whoever wishes to be great among you must be your servant" (Mark 10:44). Mary exclaimed, "He has brought down the powerful from their thrones, and lifted up the lowly" (Luke 1:52). Indeed these can be disconcerting or disturbing words to some Christians.

By taking a little child in his arms, Jesus invites us to nonviolence in a violent world. One cannot embrace war and peace at the same time. Peace is discovered in the arms that hold, not in the arms that fight. Yet war continues to devastate children's lives. A million Jewish children's lives were snuffed out in the Holocaust. How many children have died in Afghanistan and Iraq? During World War II, parents in London sent their children into the country knowing the Germans would bomb their cities. Do we have a similar attitude toward children or do we demonstrate attention deficit toward them?

Alice Miller in *The Drama of the Gifted Child* maintains that children are ideal candidates to be used by others because of their total dependence on adults. She also argues that adults who were humiliated as children will often replicate a comparable humiliation. The adult often struggles to restore the power lost in childhood. When preaching on the above text, I often ask listeners what are the characteristics of children. They respond: innocence, dependence, awe, helplessness, vulnerability, tenderness, forgiveness, and accepting others despite their race or color. They certainly have a clean slate upon which no graffiti has been smeared.

Listening to Children

We might even ask ourselves what Jesus said to the children once he took them into his arms and embraced them. Whatever it was he certainly listened to them. Fred Rogers of television's *Mister Rogers' Neighborhood* said that with the help of Margaret McFarland, a clinical psychologist, he learned really to listen to what the children were saying—through their words, their play, and their behavior.[1] We need to ask not what children can give, but what do they bring. Some considered Mr. Rogers a master when relating to children. He was, but he became this by listening and empathizing with their feelings and longings. He considered listening most important and allowed children to be themselves in his presence, and to express their fears and joys. Rogers learned to sympathize with them, especially when he recalled his own childhood experiences.

Cartoonist Charles Schulz was also able to create a world where children had fun despite fearful uncertainties. We need to be more tolerant about their temper tantrums, their inability to tie their shoes, their monsters in the bedroom, and their reluctance to go to bed at night. Rogers' approach certainly is a blueprint for us because by listening and being attuned to our children's experiences we become more attuned to their needs. He knew how to be a neighbor to children because he considered them so special. He created a neighborhood where children were treated as special and he spoke out for them.

Children need to be valued, included, and heard. Often they are unheard voices. When attentively listening to them, we might hear fear, heartbreak, or silence because of the harshness of the situation. There is a saying that grief never ends for children. They certainly don't mourn like adults and often refuse to talk about their feelings of sadness, abandonment, and loneliness. Healing, however, results when they are able to talk about their feelings.

Milwaukee state senator Gwendolynne Moore stunned a state assembly in Madison, Wisconsin, when she revealed a dark secret of her past—she was raped as a child. She has nightmares about her pedophile attacker, who took away her self-esteem and voice, and doesn't want this to happen to other children. She maintains that the power these rapists have over kids is silence. She has refused to remain silent any longer. Many children also experience violence, poverty, racism, homelessness. True love is shown by listening carefully and speaking honestly to them. It is difficult to fool children, but they can be betrayed. Children might be the smallest part of Christ's body, but they have to be listened to and welcomed. Our initial step to becoming a more just and caring community of Christians is to listen to them.

Parents need to listen more carefully to their children. One famous psychotherapist told parents that the most important thing they can provide besides food, clothing, and shelter is an attentive ear. Dr. Martin Luther King Jr. told the story of how he was driving with his father, who accidentally drove past a stop sign. A policeman pulled him over and sternly said to him, "Boy, show me your license." His father told him, "I am not a boy." Pointing to his son, he said, "This is a boy; I am a man and until you call me one, I will not listen to you." The shocked policeman nervously wrote out the ticket and quickly left. Of all the interviews that Larry King has conducted, the one he remembers most was with Dr. Martin Luther King Jr., who told him an unforgettable story. A judge one time asked Dr. King what he wanted. He responded in one word, "Respect." We show respect by attentively listening to children and others.

Jesus said, "Take care that you do not despise one of these little ones" (Matt 18:10). Because children imitate how adults act, we have an adult problem, not a child or youth problem. Thus adults become part of the problem rather than the solution. Children are aware of the hypocrisy of our leaders, teachers, and parents, who say one thing and do another. How dreadful when they put their trust in others only to be abused by them. They don't expect parents to be perfect, but they certainly want them to be honest, admit mistakes, and share how difficult it is to raise children, especially during the diaper stage. Marshal McLuhan notes that *diaper* spelled backward is *repaid*!

A good example of someone who found raising a child difficult is Edwina Gateley, who experienced a tremendous change in her life when, at the age of 49, she adopted a newborn African American child. She admitted how daunting, demanding, and challenging rearing this child became more than any other ministry she had been involved in. She wrote, "Whenever people expressed their admiration for all my ministerial achievements and my long solitary sojourns in desert and forest retreats, I knew a deeper truth. I knew that none of these courageous experiences was as stretching and brave and transformative as the day-to-day routine of raising a child."[2]

Example of Parents

Children depend on parents for love, affection, care, support, nurturing, and discipline. Parents are the child's first model of wholesome relationships. What they see will be imitated, adapted, and modeled in their future relationships. We have heard it said that the greatest gift a mother can offer to her child is to love the child's father. The same is true concerning the father. Their love created the child and has to continue to grow and be nourished. The key, of course, is commitment, which is the glue holding relationships together.

Children need to feel an integral part of the family. One way is to be given age-appropriate responsibilities for household chores. Sharing at least one meal a day when children are given an opportunity to talk about their day is very important. Katie Couric, the anchorwoman for the CBS Evening News, insists on having breakfast with her girls. They wait for her for dinner because she feels strongly that having this meal together is necessary, even if the topic of conversation is as trivial as overcooked rice. Rituals like birthdays, family gatherings, vacations, gift giving, Christmas tree trimming, and other important events need to be celebrated together. Children often comment on how important it is to spend time alone with their parents.

Cherie Blair, wife of former British Prime Minister Tony Blair, spoke at a Pontifical Academy of Social Sciences dedicated to youth in Rome in 2006. One of the points she stressed was the need for parents to carve out time from their busy schedules and invest it in conversing and listening to their children.

What message is given when parents have guns in their homes to protect themselves and allow their children to play with such weapons? Pope Benedict XVI recently gave his support to Change the Game, a project that advocates putting toy weapons aside. Since this project began, approximately forty-five hundred toy weapons have been collected. How can parents abuse tobacco and drugs, and then tell their children not to use them? When they send their children to mass but do not go with them, or have their children attend religious education classes and do not follow up, what are they teaching their children? When they make racial slurs or tell ethnic jokes, they are modeling racism. Do they expect others to teach their children manners, work ethics, and healthy habits? Parents have to "walk the walk" rather than "talk the talk."[3]

A Kaiser Family Foundation report indicates that 70 percent of children six months to six years spend at least two hours a day watching television, using computers, and playing video games. One third of them have televisions in their own rooms. Henry Shapiro, chairman of developmental and behavior pediatrics at the American Academy of Pediatrics, claims that watching television without a parent present is comparable to junk experience. Playing with toys, being read to, or spending time with adults has been replaced by television. Children watching television are usually sedentary, which then causes them to become overweight by indulging in too much junk food.[4]

Sexual Abuse

Parents often think that their children will fight the same battles they did. However, children don't because they live in a postmodern world. Children are not smaller versions of their parents but unique versions of themselves. They often do not mirror parent's beliefs, which can be disheartening to many parents.

The U.S. bishops issued a document over a decade ago called *Putting Children and Families First*. However, have bishops and priests who have strong convictions about unborn children and Catholic schools been putting children first? Or are these bishops and priests' lives actually remote from children and their families? Some bishops have failed to carry out this challenge by returning priests again into situations where sexual abuse resulted. Mistakes were made not only by bishops, but by some lawyers, therapists, and even some parents. Children who have been sexually abused and then kept this a secret have had their lives turned into turmoil. I have heard a number of times from directees, "This is the first time I have ever told this to anyone." In most instances it happened twenty, thirty, or more years ago. The darkness of this secrecy often erupts into fear, guilt, and rage, and it can have serious effects on one's health.

Sexual abuse of children, especially by clergy, religious, and church personnel, has become a scourge, a nightmare, and a pressing concern or "hot button" for all people in society. In addition, it has become an area of delicacy, embarrassment, and anguish to Catholics. Abuse goes on as well in homes by a family member or a trusted friend, but church members receive all the headlines and publicity.

Allison Turkel, a senior attorney with the National Center for Prosecution of Child Abuse, maintains in *Religion Newswriters Association* (May 13, 2002) that the Catholic Church cases are not typical, but most cases occur in the home. Archbishop Timothy Dolan of Milwaukee, Wisconsin, quoted Dr. Paul McHugh of John Hopkins University, "No one in the United States is now doing more to deal with this horror than the Catholic Church."[5] Those who have become part of the problem now have to become part of the solution. The Milwaukee Archdiocese has launched a *Safe Environment Program* that has received high praise. This program includes standards of conduct for all priests, deacons, diocesan employees, and any other church personnel involved in regular contact with children and young people. But more than money and a program are needed to alleviate the pain.

Societal costs of child abuse are startling. Studies have shown that child abuse may lead to criminal behavior later in adulthood, alcohol and drug abuse, eating disorders, spousal abuse, and high-risk sex. Some victims carry the scars with them for the rest of their lives. Studies like this necessitate a better treatment of children, adolescents, and adults who have been sexually abused. Preventive measures are of prime importance in all communities. Parents need to educate themselves about abuse and warn their children about it. Above all, they need to listen to their children when something doesn't sound right. The good news is that, according to the national media, the majority of Catholics still love their church. They, however, want accountability by insisting that priest child molesters be turned over to legal authorities.

Justice toward Children

The number of children suffering from disease, especially AIDS, is a justice issue. Some fifteen million have lost one or both of their parents due to this disease. One in eight have been orphaned in sub-Sahara Africa. It is estimated that by 2010, there will be forty million orphans in Africa, India, and China. Education is necessary to break the cycle of HIV/AIDS, illiteracy, hunger, and excruciating poverty.[6]

Sierra Leone, a West African country, has the highest infant mortality rate in the world. One out of three children attend school. Clean water and health care are scarce commodities. In the 1990s, ten thousand children were conscripted as soldiers because of a civil war that had been raging for eleven years. These children were also required to kill a family member to guarantee that they could never return to their home village. Addressing the needs of Sierra Leone, Matthias Seisay, who is from that country and is presently studying at Marquette University in Milwaukee, Wisconsin, has founded a legal service to protect children suffering from human rights abuses. He saves bikes from scrap heaps, schools, and police stations, and sends them to children in Sierra Leone. He said that the children there consider them a treasure.

In May 2002, the United Nations addressed the problem of justice toward children. Former Secretary General Kofi Annan stated, "We are meeting here because there is no issue more unifying, more urgent, or more universal than the welfare of our children. There is no issue more important."[7] The amazing part of this conference was how children and young people told their stories about their encounters with violence, poverty, physical and sexual abuse, disease, and imprisonment. They shared their vision for a better world for children because this dream will be a better world for everyone. They called upon adults to accept their responsibility for the poor children in the world and provide the needed action to secure a better future. So what will we do, sit idly in front of our televisions cursing the darkness or be lights dispelling the shadows of evil?

Parents can't possibly shield their children from all dangers, but they can offer their best effort in raising them. We have a knowledge explosion in which computers have taken the place of crayons for children. However, it is unjust that some parents are placing a higher priority on their own happiness than on their children's. Most parents believe that raising children is far more difficult than in the past. Jesus said, "Is there anyone among you who, if your child asks for a fish, will give a snake instead of a fish? Or if the child asks for an egg, will you give him a scorpion? If you then, who are evil, know how to give good gifts to your children, how much more will the heavenly Father give the Holy Spirit to those who ask him!" (Luke 11:11–13).

When children embrace unfamiliar interests or explore talents different from their mother or father, the parents are often disappointed. It becomes a challenge to love them as the prodigal father loved his son when he showed his independence. Also, some parents still suffer from the wounds inflicted on them from their parents. Trying to shield their children from all harm is as futile as getting a rooster to lay an egg or cutting a rock with a razor blade. Parents need to tell them how much they love their children over and over, which will prove what Saint Paul insisted, that love never fails.

Greatest in the Kingdom

Jesus said, "Truly I tell you, unless you change and become like children, you will never enter the kingdom of heaven. Whoever becomes humble like this child is the greatest in the kingdom of heaven" (Matt 18:3–4). Jesus instructs his disciples on what it means to belong to the assembly of believers or to enter the kingdom of heaven. He responds by addressing the unasked question of what is necessary to be a child in the kingdom. So he enacts a parable by putting a small child in their midst. The model is certainly simple, but the lesson is far more complicated. Here we are presented with some ground rules on how to live in community with one another as well as how to discipline oneself, especially in the area of forgiving. Jesus admonished his followers to change their attention from greatness of wanting to be first to paying more attention to other-centeredness that becomes the heart of community life. This leads to the question: Did Jesus declare here that he would always remain a child or childlike?

We need to remind ourselves that children in Jesus' time did not have any social status. They were unable to discuss the Torah. So how can a child be a model for entering the kingdom? That is the challenge Jesus offers us because to become a child means to put aside our status and accept our vulnerability and powerlessness. Are we willing to do that? Jesus wants us to be more childlike, not to act in childish ways where we can't admit a mistake. Our spiritual lives feel wafer thin at times. We find it hard to accept how fragile we are, as fragile as a spider's web or snowflake, when we want to be a marble statue. We find it difficult when our plans, progress, and projects bring little results or success. Turning away from self-sufficiency and depending more on God is daunting. Prestige, pride, and self-importance need to be replaced with humility; exclusivity needs to give way to inclusiveness, especially of the marginalized. Saint Paul eventually realized that God's grace was sufficient for him in his weakness and powerlessness. He stated, "I will boast all the more gladly of my weaknesses, so that the power of Christ may dwell in me. Therefore I am content with weaknesses, insults, hardships, persecutions, and calamities for the sake of Christ; for when I am weak, then I am strong" (2 Cor 12:9–10). The atom of our weakness or powerlessness split by omnipotence or the Spirit can unleash tremendous power.

A Little Child Will Guide Them

Isaiah exclaimed "a little child shall lead them" to everlasting peace (Isa 11:6). Our government's "No Child Left Behind" policy does not seem to be a priority, and we deceive ourselves if we think it is. Why did our welfare system in 1995 require single mothers of small children to get a job? The result was many latchkey children. How do we explain that in Oregon the state cut seventeen days from the school year due to funding issues while our government is willing to finance an Iraq war? How do we justify cuts in Medicaid resulting in millions of poor children who will not be able to visit a doctor?[8] They truly are the poorest of the poor, the "least of the least"! These are not rhetorical questions that we ask ourselves but questions that need answers. Every day thirty-seven thousand children die. Every 3.5 seconds a child dies because of starvation or from a lack of basic medical care. One pastor had his congregation snap their fingers every three seconds to get his point across. Try it, and the impact is evident!

Anne Dillard reminds us in *For the Time Being* that half of all the dead in human history are children. We hear the cry of Jeremiah, "They know no limits in their deeds of wickedness; they do not judge with justice the cause of the orphan, to make it proper, and they do not defend the rights of the needy" (Jer 5:28). We read in Exodus concerning orphans, "You shall not abuse any widow or orphan. If you do abuse them when they cry out me, I will certainly hear their cry" (Exod 22:22). How much more so will God hear the children who are the least vocal of our neighbors?

In 2 Kings 5:1–19, we have the story of Naaman, who contracted leprosy. His military prowess suddenly disappears and he is forced to face his vulnerability. It is a slave girl, a worthless one, however, who acts in God's name. She says to her mistress, "If only my lord were with the prophet who is in Samaria! He would cure him of his leprosy" (v. 3). She was able to influence Naaman and help him to be cleansed of his leprosy.

Another story about children in a rescuing situation is found in John (6:1–14). Jesus asks Philip how are they going to feed the large crowd that had gathered to listen to Jesus. Andrew comes to the rescue by informing Jesus that there is a boy there who has five barley loaves and two fish. Andrew, as well as Philip, might have said later to the boy, "Thanks, kid, you saved our lives!" We marvel how children live in the present moment and how spontaneous and loving they are.

One cannot predict what children will say at times. I remember being invited by a family for a meal at their house. At the end of the meal the four-year-old girl piped up, "Mommy, daddy, why don't we invite Father to come more often? We get better meals." A teacher asked her small children who God was. One small boy said, "I know who God is! God is whatever you think he is, but he is not a girl."

If children present the hope for a better future, we need to pay closer attention to them. They are beautiful not only on the outside but especially on the inside. We face a real crisis in the care and health of our young, especially when we lower standards of Head Start programs and reduce similar initiatives. Who will speak for the children?

Jesus was well aware of their plight and reached out to them. Fred Rogers did a marvelous job. Are we contributing to or alleviating our children's crises? Will the time come when the church can offer a model on how to deal with sexual abuse of children? We are going through our Good Friday, and maybe we should return to Holy Thursday, which stresses servant leadership. We need to discover ways to speak and act on behalf of children. As Christians we need to lead the way to help and heal—truly a challenging adventure.

𖣚 𖣚 𖣚

SCRIPTURE PASSAGES FOR REFLECTION

"Whoever welcomes this child in my name welcomes me, and whoever welcomes me welcomes the one who sent me; for the least among all of you is the greatest." (Luke 9:48)

"Whoever wishes to be great among you must be your servant." (Mark 10:44)

"Is there anyone among you who, if your child asks for a fish, will give a snake instead of a fish?" (Luke 11:11)

"Truly I tell you, unless you change and become like children, you will never enter the kingdom of heaven." (Matt 18:3).

"A little child will lead them." (Isa 11:6)

QUESTIONS TO CONSIDER

1. How can we speak for children, especially those used by others for their selfish purposes?

2. What will enable us to listen more closely to them?

3. How can we set a better example for them to imitate?

4. Are there other ways to address sexual abuse and infant mortality?

5. What can be done to alleviate the fact that every three seconds a child dies?

12

BECOMING *"A PRAY-ER"*

"Father if you are willing, remove this cup from me;
yet, not my will but yours be done."
Luke 22:42

Maybe the greatest challenge for any Christian is to immerse oneself deeply in prayer and become *"a pray-er."* George Herbert, a poet, likened it to God's breath or the soul's blood. Our whole lives should be a prayer if we are in union with God who first loved us.

Prayer is a love encounter. In prayer, two lives intersect much like two lovers. Karl Rahner maintains that it is impossible not to pray if we know how to love. Martin Buber states that prayer is a much deeper encounter than marriage, which explains why the saints could spend so much time in prayer. They made room for someone greater than themselves. The struggle required in this process is comparable to Jacob's struggle with the angel (cf. Gen 32:23–25), which left him a better person, although he had to limp through life. Job and Jonah had similar struggles and were purified because of them. Jesus struggled in the garden of Gethsemane, praying to have the cup taken away, but adding, "not my will but yours be done" (Luke 22:42). Kazantzakis, a Greek philosopher and writer, insisted that there is no better dis- cipline than wrestling with God. Saint Francis of Assisi wrestled with God and became an outstanding saint who is deeply revered by all. The difference between ourselves and the saints is that we circle around the fire to warm ourselves, whereas the saints threw themselves into the fire of divine love and then spread that love.

Prayer means a forgetting of oneself. If we are honest with ourselves, we will have to admit there is too much of self or ego in us, our plans, projects, and problems. Ego could mean edging God out, and that is what a selfish person does. Greek philosophers used to teach that our greatest conquest is ourselves. It is told of Alexander the Great that one day, in a fit of rage, he killed a man. Here was a man who had conquered the whole world of his time, but he could not conquer himself. Jesus said it well, "For where your treasure is, there your heart will be also" (Matt 6:21). What do we think about most? Usually our thoughts center around ourselves and our plans.

In prayer, we allow God to seek us. Too often, we imagine prayer as what we do, that we initiate it. Prayer has to become less and less of what we do, and more and more what God does. God wants to pray in, with, and through us, so we need to get out of the way. We don't pray to make God aware of us, but we pray to help us better understand God's presence in our lives. In prayer, we are touched deeply by God and an enriching of a relationship results. Prayer should not be an obligation or something that we have to do. This is expressed at times as "I didn't say my morning prayers or my rosary." We have trouble with prayer because we have to work harder at praying. We need to allow God to become more intimate with us because we still have not grasped how much God loves us. God is fond of us, but do we blush when God tells us? Our problem is that we are not sure God wants to be so intimate with us. We need to open up our hearts so we can hear God say to us, "I love you." "You are precious." Once we absorb these words, or devour them like Ezekiel eating the scroll, these tender thoughts can change our lives.

The Spirit can show us how to pray as Saint Paul wrote: "Likewise the Spirit helps us in our weakness; for we do not know how to pray as we ought, but that very Spirit intercedes with sighs too deep for words" (Rom 8:26). We need to be led by the Spirit as Jesus was and open our hearts to a loving God. Then our prayer becomes dynamic and not static. There will be highs and lows, ebbs and flows, just as there are in any love relationship. In prayer we can grow beyond a human relationship if we are willing. Prayer has to be based on a spirituality of attitudes, values, and a deepening of a relationship, rather than exercises and functions.

Jesus tells us how to pray, "When you are praying, do not heap up empty phrases as the Gentiles do; for they think that they will be heard because of their many words. Do not be like them" (Matt 6:7–8). It is possible to say a lot of prayers without really praying. Jesus quotes Isaiah as saying, "This people honors me with their lips, but their hearts are far from me" (Matt 15:8). Some people even brag how many rosaries they say, maintaining the more the better. I remember one parish where the people recited the rosary before mass, and had only so much time to finish it. They were rattling off the Hail Mary's so fast that you could not understand what they were saying.

Distractions

Spiritual masters tell us that in prayer we need to concentrate, be attentive, and be aware of God's loving presence. Daydreaming or following a stream of consciousness is not prayer, but distractions are often part of our prayer and do upset us. Cardinal Newman admitted that we are often distracted and disordered at prayer. Experts point out that we cannot concentrate more than a few seconds on anything without a distraction. That applies to our prayer life as well. Saint Francis de Sales would often spend his time in prayer fighting off the distractions. Saint Aloysius resolved to persist in prayer so that he could pray one hour without a distraction. Do you wonder if he ever made it? Saint Theresa shook her hourglass that the time would go faster. We read in the Book of Daniel that when he started out his prayer, "the prince of the kingdom of Persia opposed me for twenty-one days. So Michael, one of the chief princes, came to help me" (Dan 10:13). God assured Daniel that his prayer was heard.

The causes of distractions are many: ill health, human weakness, fatigue, cluttered minds, to name a few. Someone described our minds as mills that are very noisy, but the mills don't stop functioning because of the noise. Probably one of the best ways to counteract the distractions is to pray them or find God in them. So if we are distracted by a plane flying overhead, say a prayer for the pilot and the passengers that they arrive safely at their destination. Another way is to clear our minds, before we pray, of the business or activity that we might be engaged in. Our minds can sometimes act like busy bees fluttering from one flower to another. The trouble is that the bees are more successful. Some suggest that another way to deal with distractions is to laugh at them, especially crazy ones. Some of us have many of those.

No Time

Christians will often say that they haven't got the time to pray because they are so busy. If we don't have time to pray, then we are *too* busy. Jesus found time to pray, as depicted in Luke's Gospel, where you will find at least fourteen passages dealing with Jesus and prayer. If he had to pray, then how much more ourselves?

We often are stressed out or tired at the end of our day: rising early, eating a quick breakfast, fighting traffic, engaging in boring work, wolfing down a lunch, fighting more traffic, getting home and tending to loved ones, having a meal, and then maybe having to attend a meeting. Hard as this is, we need to find time to pray, and it doesn't have to be a long period of time. One of the greatest enemies of prayer is neglect. I remember a religious sister telling me that she was so busy in her ministry that she just could not find time to pray. As she continued to talk, I found out that she was reading novels and watching a lot of television. Prayer had not become a priority in her life, and until it did she probably would find all kinds of excuses not to pray, as some of us do. In *Deus Caritas Est*, Pope Benedict XVI writes that prayer is a means of drawing new strength from Christ and is urgently needed in our lives. He uses Mother Teresa of Calcutta as an example of someone devoted to God in prayer and service to others (no. 36).

Involvement in our work is often the enemy of prayer, especially when it is urgent. There is a tyranny of the urgent. We are so busy; but as Thoreau, a philosopher and famous author, wrote, if we are so busy, what are we so busy about? The constant whirlpool of activity will divert our attention to what we consider pressing matters. Besides, we receive far more aesthetic satisfaction when we finish a task than when we spend an hour in prayer. We have to get certain projects done, but this same urgency is not always present in prayer.

Correcting papers for class is far more noticeable than spending an hour in prayer. Just as the Letter of James warns us against faith without works, we need to guard against activism without a prayer life. We can easily evaluate our effectiveness by the world's criteria. Prayer essentially is an inward journey to silence, an intimate union with God, where we find our deeper selves and how imperfect we are but still loved by God. Many of us, however, prefer not to engage in that journey but rather indulge is some other activity.

We sometimes procrastinate and keep putting prayer off, secretly hoping that something will come up to absorb our time. Paul advocated, "Pray in the Spirit at all times in every prayer and supplication" (Eph 6:18). Recall how Jesus told his disciples, "Come away to a deserted place all by yourselves and rest a while. For many were coming and going, and they had no leisure even to eat. And they went away in the boat to a deserted place by themselves" (Mark 6:31–32). Doesn't this sound familiar? Jesus invites us to do the same, but do we respond? Temptations not to pray are the easiest to overcome.

Thomas More had the custom of getting up at three in the morning and praying until six. For more than fifty years, Bishop Fulton Sheen spent a holy hour in prayer and attributed his outstanding teaching and preaching success to that. Some of the most active saints, including Augustine, Thomas Aquinas, Vincent de Paul, Mother Frances Cabrini, and Mother Teresa of Calcutta, found the time to pray despite their busy lives. Saint Francis of Assisi's favorite expression was "My God and my All," which he discovered through many hours of prayer. God should receive the best part of our day. Is that happening?

Often people tell me that when they pray they fall asleep. Welcome aboard! Saint Thomas Aquinas, a prolific writer, wrote that if we go into prayer with the intention of praying and fall asleep, that is still considered a good prayer. Three cheers for Saint Thomas! However, it is important not to pray when we are tired, otherwise our prayer becomes an endurance contest. The story is told of a group of religious who had their meditation period at 5:30 a.m. During that time period, one of the friars fell asleep and started to snore. Thank goodness the local minister had a sense of humor. He bellowed out, "Stop it, stop it, you will wake the others." If we happen to sleep, try to accept the fact that we are human. Remember Jesus in the Garden of Olives and how he found his apostles sleeping. He said to them, "Why are you sleeping? Get up and pray that you may not come into the time of trial" (Luke 22:46).

Difficulty Praying

Christians suffering a traumatic experience in their lives such as divorce, sexual abuse, death of a loved one, loss of a job, or being told that they have terminal disease will find it hard to pray. At these crisis moments, we often feel powerless, hopeless, vulnerable, and out of control. We can experience a living nightmare and might more readily identify with Job's and Saint Paul's sleepless nights. We might feel that God has abandoned us, that we are lost and forsaken. Hard as it is, we need to cry out with the psalmist, "Out of the depths I cry to you, O Lord. Lord, hear my voice" (Ps 130:1).

Ronald Rolheiser, OMI, a specialist in systematic theology and spirituality, admits: "Too often when we try to pray when hurting, the prayer serves not to uproot the hurt and the narcissism, but to root it even more deeply in self-pity, self-preoccupation, and darkness."[1] He suggests that we focus more on God than on ourselves. God is still with us in many ways, perhaps in a family member, a friend, or someone taking care of us like a doctor or a nurse, or a priest who came to visit us. God will never abandon us. Prayers of desperation when darkness sets in become a doorway to God's love and compassion. More courage is needed to face the darkness than the light. We often end up hugging the guardrails rather than God. We desire solid ground beneath us rather than quaking earth. We need to be reminded that God is present at this intense time, this breaking point, the eye of the storm. We like the apostles have to pray, "Lord, save us."

Spiritual aridity can set in as it did for many of the saints, like John of the Cross and Teresa of Avila, but they remained faithful in prayer and became outstanding mystics. Prayer is often like the seasons. At times, we find little consolation in prayer that has become empty and dry. Even our ministry or relationships lack any kind of spark. When experiencing dry periods, we have to guard against feeling like a failure. Ironically, God becomes most present when we are most empty. We need to remain faithful to our prayer at these times because God might be calling us to a higher form of prayer. Some of the signs are being unable to meditate and taking no pleasure in using the imagination. But if, despite this, we delight in being alone with God, we may be called to contemplation, rather than meditation. It is so easy to give up prayer when it becomes blah, or to return to our former way of praying. Saint Paul encourages us, "Pray without ceasing" (1 Thess 5:17). Maybe we need to recite one of Teresa of Avila's poems:

Let nothing disturb you;
Let nothing make you afraid;
All things pass;
But God is unchanging.[2]

Sister Ann Shields, SGL, tells of her experience of spiritual dryness in prayer that lasted for four years. No matter what she tried, nothing seemed to help. The Lord kept telling her that you decrease; I increase. Finally, she yielded to this invitation and experienced countless blessings because God became the center of her life and she had to let go of trying to control situations.

What a beautiful motto for a Christian: He must increase, and I must decrease.

God is present in our emptiness and desolation. God will feed us, as was evident to the Israelites out in the desert. Elijah was very discouraged and fled out into the desert because Jezebel wanted to kill him. God sent him an angel to feed him and "He got up, and ate and drank; then he went in the strength of that food forty days and forty nights to Horeb the mount of God" (1 Kgs 19:8). Jesus fed five thousand people in the desert, and he was comforted by an angel in the garden of Gethsemane as "his sweat became like great drops of blood falling down on the ground" (Luke 22:44). If our faith is deep enough, we also are fed and strengthened in times of spiritual aridity. We can't give up when we experience battle fatigue.

Restlessness

Our spiritual antennae are sometimes not in contact with God. This lack of reception can be caused by boredom, loneliness, fear, anxiety, restlessness. We often counteract these feelings by keeping ourselves busy, overeating, drinking too much, watching a lot of television, or playing games on the computer. These and similar activities, however, do not satisfy our restlessness. We need to realign our spiritual antennae because something is missing in our lives. Saint Augustine expressed it well when he wrote that our hearts are restless until they rest in God.

In *Pray and Never Lose Heart* Sister Ann Shields relates how Heather Cuthrell, a laywoman of Long Beach, California, spends an hour a day in prayer. She claims that she has much more calm because she knows that God has a hand in whatever happens, and that helps her not to become uptight about things. Many laypeople spend extra time daily in prayer and have found how beneficial prayer has been in developing their spiritual lives. Truly they are an inspiration, especially those who take the time out from their busy schedules to make an annual retreat.

According to Thomas Merton, contemplative prayer is the answer to restlessness. It took him many years to find out what contemplation and solitude can do in his life. Contemplation, according to John of the Cross, is the highest form of prayer because it involves "loving attention." Mystics like him and Teresa of Avila fell in love with God passionately through contemplative prayer. They committed themselves to a journey that never got there. They realized that the spiritual life is a continual discovery of God in places we never expected to find God. That might include people we don't like or things we hate to do. Contemplation is an invitation to go inward so we can share outward. Space scientists explore the outer limits, the mystics the inner limits.

G. K. Chesterton used the image about Saint Francis seeing the world upside down. Every encounter with God deepened the saints' hunger and thirst for a more satisfying interior life. Jan Walgrave, a Dominican scholar, believes that there is a conspiracy against the interior life. The inability to develop an interior life becomes rather obvious when people find it uncomfortable to be in silence and solitude. When some Christians desire to make a weekend retreat at a center and find out that it is a silent retreat, some will exclaim: "I don't know if I can keep quiet that long." Thomas Merton wrote: "It is in deep solitude that I find the gentleness with which I can truly love my brothers. The more solitary I am the more affection I have for them. It is pure affection and filled with reverence for the solitude of others."[3]

Unanswered Prayers

People have told me that they pray and pray, but God does not hear or answer them. Then we don't believe what Jesus said, "Ask and it will be given you; search and you will find; knock, and the door will be opened to you. For everyone who asks receives, and everyone who searches finds, and for everyone who knocks, the door will be opened" (Luke 11:9–10).

Remember how long Augustine's mother prayed for the conversion of her son, some twenty years. She became what she did not ask for, Saint Monica. I will never forget the mother who asked me, "Do you know how long I have prayed for my son to come back?"

I replied, "No."

She said, "Forty years, and he finally converted."

Jesus said, "If in my name you ask me for anything, I will do it" (John 14:14). Even if we ask Jesus for a thimble of help, he will give us an ocean for our request. Sometimes, however, God says no; so we have to ask ourselves can we accept it? A no from God is just as creative as a yes. Who knows what is best for us, God or ourselves? To wish for every prayer to be answered is a recipe for disaster. All prayers are answered, but maybe not in the way we want them.

This truth is brought out by a man at a beach who was watching how the children kept coming to their parents asking for some soda. All they received was a hug and some water. It reminded him how God responds to our requests, but maybe not exactly the way we want. As Saint James points out, "You ask and do not receive, because you ask wrongly" (Jas 4:3). We need to pray for what God wants, not what we want. In every request, we need to add, "Not my will but yours be done." This is the hardest way to pray, especially if we readily accept what happens.

The secret of all prayer is perseverance. Recall the widow who wanted the judge to render a just decision for her. He refused for a long time, but she kept pestering him and finally said, "Because this widow keeps bothering me, I will grant her justice" (Luke 18:5). Maybe the reason our prayers are not heard is that we have not forgiven someone or are holding a grudge. Grudges don't improve by harboring them. Jesus said, "So when you are offering your gift at the altar, if you remember that your brother or sister has something against you, leave your gift there before the altar and go; first be reconciled to your brother or sister, and then come and offer your gift" (Matt 5:23–24). Imagine what could happen if more Christians did this!

Prayer is a matter of waiting. Like the psalmist said, "I waited patiently for the Lord; he inclined to me and heard my cry" (Ps 40:1) or "Our soul waits for the Lord; he is our help and shield" (Ps 33:20). It is comparable to the pregnant woman who said that all she had to do was wait. Waiting can be monotonous and distasteful. We often want quick results and fast relief—we even put a stopwatch on a headache. We want immediate gratification; we have instant coffee, instant tea, why not instant spirituality?

The story is told that Saint Scholastica used to visit her twin brother Saint Benedict once a year. They met in a farmhouse near his monastery, spending the time in prayer and spiritual matters. Realizing that she was near death, she pleaded with Benedict to stay with her an extra day. Not wanting to stay away from his monastery, he refused. Scholastica asked God for the favor, and shortly thereafter a severe thunderstorm broke out which prevented Benedict from returning. He cried out, "God forgive you, Sister. What have you done?" She replied, "I asked a favor of you and you refused. I asked it of God and he granted it."[4]

Listening

Prayer is also a matter of listening. Catherine de Hueck Doherty, foundress of Madonna House, considered listening to the Holy Spirit as the essence of prayer. Listening is a forgotten art in our society. Almost half of our day seems to be spent in listening, but how much do we really listen?

One of the reasons Jesus was so effective in his ministry was because he actively listened to the Father and others. Did not the Father say at the transfiguration, "This is my Son, the beloved; with him I am well pleased; listen to him!" (Matt 17:5). When we actively listen to others, we listen not just with our head but with our heart. We listen not just to what the person says, but to what the person doesn't say. Sometimes what the person does not say is more important than what the person says. It becomes a dying and rising process. Jesus said, "Unless a grain of wheat falls into the earth and dies, it remains just a single grain, but if it dies, it bears much fruit" (John 12:24). Listening is a dying process, and our prayer life will be more fruitful to the extent that we listen. The dying process is difficult because God may allow us to stay in the tomb while we are clamoring to get out on the first day.

Recall how Samuel was called in the middle of the night. He thought it was Eli calling him. But Eli said, "I did not call." This happened three times, and finally Eli told him to say, "Speak, for your servant is listening," which Samuel did (1 Sam 3:1–10). Yet, what do we do? We say, "Listen, Lord, for your servant speaks!" Elijah was told by God to stand on the mountain because the Lord would pass by. A strong wind arose, but the Lord was not in the wind. Then an earthquake and then fire, but the Lord was not in either, but in "a sound of sheer silence" (1 Kgs 19:11–12).

God can speak to us in silence because silence is God's language. We find it hard, however, to deal with silence and solitude. Silence can overcome our business and our lives, which are often permeated with noise. God's silence during the crucifixion is excruciating because evil seems to triumph, but it doesn't and never will. If we can't accept a friend's silence, it probably will be more difficult to accept a friend's words. When God is silent, that might be the beginning of prayer. Some people will say, "I listen, but God doesn't say anything." Then we have not listened, because God has spoken in his Word and everything else is an echo.

Praying Feelings

What I find in conducting directed retreats and being a companion in spiritual direction is that directees often don't pray their feelings. Many of us have a tendency to express our feelings to others by talking behind peoples' backs, making snide and cynical remarks, shouting outbursts of anger, or seeking revenge. We don't feel comfortable about telling God how dissipated, bored, tired, bitter, or angry we might be. So we pray some other thoughts. This is the time we need to be brutally honest with God, as Tevyé was in *Fiddler on the Roof*. He sang his frustration. If we are angry at God, God will not strike us dead, but will understand like a loving mother or father for their child who has an occasional tantrum.

Most of us are hurting but the question remains where are we hurting? Is it from rejection, humiliation, disappointment, or some indignity that results in bitterness, coldness, cynicism, and anger? We often say when asked how we are that we are fine. Actually, our hearts are bleeding and our fists are clenched. At these times, we need to enter into our own brokenness, restlessness, and inadequacies by having recourse to prayer. Prayer often brings us peace of mind and helps us to surrender to a loving and understanding God.

We have to admit that we are not always kind, thoughtful, loving, compassionate, and hopeful. It might not be easy to admit in prayer that we are selfish but we need to take whatever is going on in our lives into prayer. If we are angry, bored, sexually obsessed, tired, then pray that. Following this advice makes it much easier to "pray always." We need to be anchored in who we are, whether married, single, religious, deacon, priest, or bishop. This awareness, as Anthony de Mello, SJ, a psychotherapist and spiritual writer, points out, will prevent us from sleepwalking through life and will enhance our prayer.

Jean Gill, a spiritual director, writes: "Feelings surface from deep within our Self and express the movement of the Spirit. They present our true and authentic Self, not who we think we are or should be in a given situation. When we allow any and all of our emotions to surface uncensored and then experience them fully until they are spent, we engage ourselves with the life and movement of the Spirit within. We are likely to come to a calmer place…When we let go and sink deeply into the feelings moving in the situation, we let God do the work, and we open our self to the wisdom and truth of the Spirit revealed within the experience."[5]

The effects of battling spiritual aridity, distractions, restlessness, unanswered prayers, and not listening or praying our feelings will result in, as Cardinal Newman maintained, a deeper union with God, knowing God's will, interior transformation, and a subjection of our passions. Pope Benedict XVI uses Mother Teresa of Calcutta as an example of someone who was immersed in prayer. She wrote a letter to her coworker in 1996 stating that we need a deep connection with God in our daily lives. And the best way, she insisted, is through prayer.

Prayer has more to do with communion than communication. We need to go deeply inward to be able to share better outwardly. Teresa of Avila spoke of the seventh mansion where we experience God directly. John of the Cross spoke of it as the unitive way. Ruth Burrows calls it the third island, and Anna Dillard as going into the matrix, the pit of our soul.

Prayer should lead us to the most profound acts of love, reaching out to others, caring, sharing our lives. Prayer needs to permeate all we do. The secret of praying well is to pray often. How else can his kingdom come as we pray in the Our Father? Frequent and deep prayer will change us to live more virtuous lives reaching out to others who are in much greater need, and that is how we become *"a pray-er."*

⚜　⚜　⚜

SCRIPTURE PASSAGES FOR REFLECTION

"Come away to a deserted place all by yourselves and rest a while. For many were coming and going, and they had no leisure even to eat." (Mark 6:31)

"Ask and it will be given you; search, and you will find; knock, and the door will be opened for you." (Luke 11:9)

"When you are praying, do not heap up empty phrases as the Gentiles do." (Matt 6:7)

"Likewise the Spirit helps in our weakness; for we do not know how to pray as we ought, but that very Spirit intercedes with sighs too deep for words." (Rom 8:26)

"Pray without ceasing." (1 Thess 5:17)

QUESTIONS TO CONSIDER

1. How do we handle or deal with distractions in prayer?

2. How can we find the time to pray with a busy schedule?

3. What are the times that we find it hard to pray and how do we handle them?

4. When do we find silence, contemplation, and listening difficult?

5. How do we respond to unanswered prayers?

6. Do we understand the importance of praying our feelings? Have we learned to do this?

CONCLUDING THOUGHTS

As we come to the end of this book, we may now be in a better position to answer the question: How Christian are we? It is far more challenging to be a disciple of Jesus than a follower. Do we have a better understanding of how much God loves us, especially after reading Pope Benedict XVI's encyclical, *Deus Caritas Est* ("God is Love")? We have to admit that we need more love than we truly deserve. God's love for us is everlasting, unconditional, no strings attached, and based on nothing. We probably would blush if we felt deeply how much God loves us. We need a wide-angle lens to more fully appreciate God's love. God takes delight in us as a mother takes delight in her child.

It makes good sense to put God first in our lives and our neighbor next. Love of God and love of neighbor cannot exist without the other as Pope Benedict XVI points out in his encyclical. We become more human by being for others. Our challenge is to remove the barriers between ourselves and our neighbors and not to become closeted within ourselves. Our greatest passion must be our compassion for our neighbors and spending less time discussing and theorizing how helping them is to be done. We have to put on the armor of God because we have work to do.

Discipline plays an important role in living the Christian life, especially in our creature comfort society. We need to discipline ourselves so that we do not become self-centered, distant, or casual in our relationship with others. Delayed satisfaction and

making a decision ahead of time are the price of true discipleship. We are challenged to overcome the same temptations Jesus
experienced—materialism, power, and sensationalism—which
then leads us to the freedom Jesus exemplified. It takes much
discipline to realize that the teachings and values of Christ take
precedence over everything else. We need to raise our consciousness of who Jesus is in our lives.

As Christians, we need to move beyond tolerance because too
many forms of hatred exist in our society. Even our dark side can
be ingredients for an authentic, healthy spirituality, and it can
lead us to uncharted waters. Experiencing darkness, suffering,
and pain can lead to freedom and joy. Demonstrating a better
understanding of religious traditions and tearing down the walls
and fences of intolerance can be daunting. We are challenged to
protest all animosities and divisions. Violence and hatred leading
to enmity are certainly part of our daily news. Besides overcoming the various *isms,* more clever ones exist, such as dishonest
corporations, scapegoating, and conflicts in the church. We need
to *care-front* people who are intolerant of others, harboring violence and enmity. Jesus *care-fronted* the rich young man searching
for eternal life. He also *care-fronts* us out of our comfortable
lifestyles, especially our interests that run contrary to Jesus
Christ. *Care-frontation* is one of the more difficult gospel counsels
to carry out, but the benefits far outweigh the difficulties and cannot be measured on any scale.

We might take pride in giving to charitable causes or to our
respective place of worship, but how forgiving are we? By taking
the initiative in forgiving we show the highest kind of love, the
love that Pope Benedict writes about in his encyclical. We need
to let go of any hurts as Jesus did, and be able to forgive others
and ourselves of our past. Wrapping ourselves in a mantle of forgiveness will indicate what kind of Christian we are.

A positive attitude will help us to deal with many of the harsh realities we face. A positive attitude is more important than aptitude because it will determine our altitude in life. It will counteract stress, the roller coaster of emotions we all face, and make us more joyful and peaceful. A positive attitude will enable us to follow Jesus down the road of sacrifice and service. The dint of hard work in acquiring a positive attitude will result in much self-improvement.

How to deal with wealth can be a high wire act and far more challenging than dealing with sex or politics. The injustice arises when people are unwilling to share. When money becomes a false god and greed pervades our lives, the gap between the rich and poor widens, and other peoples' needs will not be met. Poor people become outsiders. We can become enmeshed in structures that keep others poor. Do we spend lots of money on clothes only to clothe our inner nakedness? The story of the rich man and Lazarus continues to be reenacted. The poor are neglected, forgotten, and become invisible in our society. Whom do we exclude from our lives or consider outsiders? Children are often treated as outsiders. We need to listen more to their needs, set better examples for them, and address the problems of sexual abuse and infant mortality. Our words have to match our deeds.

Jesus calls us to a radical and holy life. Like the apostles, we are stumblers and slow learners when it comes to prayer. One of our greatest challenges is becoming *"a pray-er"* by praying more frequently and overcoming its obstacles: not having time, distractions, spiritual aridity, unanswered prayers. A deepening of our prayer life will definitely help us to become better Christians.

A Twelve-Point Checklist

HOW TO BECOME A BETTER CHRISTIAN

"Be perfect, therefore, as your heavenly Father is perfect."
Matt 5:48

1. I can say that I feel deeply loved by God, which has changed my life.
2. I have regularly acted as a Good Samaritan regardless of whom the recipient might be.
3. I have become more disciplined and self-controlled by overcoming materialism and consumerism, and by living a simple lifestyle.
4. I have moved beyond tolerance and found a balance between it and intolerance.
5. I do not use harsh words or build up walls of hate and animosity, I refrain from scapegoating, and I am willing to turn the other cheek.
6. I *care-front* others and myself despite being afraid at times by creating a proper climate and doing it with an understanding heart.

7. I have forgiven others who have hurt me, allowing my greatest hurt to become my greatest blessing, and I have forgiven myself of my past.

8. I possess a positive attitude despite all the trials, disappointments, and hardships that I have experienced.

9. I share my wealth, talent, treasure, and time for the good of others, especially the marginalized.

10. I try not to exclude anyone from my life, especially people who are homeless, poor, have HIV virus or AIDS, homosexuals, lesbians, orphans, prisoners, and undocumented immigrants.

11. I have a great respect and love for children, and I make an effort to listen to them and set a good example.

12. I am faithful to my prayer life, making it a priority in my life despite distractions, business, spiritual aridity, and unanswered prayers.

NOTES

Chapter 1. God Our Lover

1. A phrase used by Pope John Paul II.

2. Peter Van Breemen, SJ, *The God Who Won't Let Go* (Notre Dame, IN: Ave Maria Press, 2001), 28.

3. Gerald May, *The Dark Night of the Soul* (San Francisco, CA: Harper, 2004), 50.

4. William Sloane Coffin, *Credo* (Louisville, KY: John Knox Press, 2004), 154.

5. Michael Ford, ed., *Eternal Seasons: A Liturgical Journey with Henri J.M. Nouwen* (Notre Dame, IN: Sorin Books, 2004), 109.

6. E. Ann Hillestad, "Offering the Good News" *America* (20 February 2006): 19–21.

7. He has written *Are You Serious?* in which he tells us how God's love and mercy changed his life and how we need to take God seriously.

Chapter 2. Who Is My Neighbor?

1. James F. Keenan, SJ, "The Neighbor in Luke and Matthew" *The Living Pulpit* 11, no. 3 (2002): 9.

2. She has written at least five books relating to gender, sex, hate speech, and the limits of self-knowledge.

3. Each year Jimmy and Rosalyn Carter give a week of their time to build homes. They have gone to India and Africa.

4. Harold Dean Trulear, "Conquering Space: Mister Roger's Neighborhood" *The Living Pulpit* 11, no. 3 (2002): 10–11.

5. Susan Blum Gerding, "Six Steps to Effective Evangelization," in *John Paul II and the New Evangelization,* eds. Ralph Martin and Peter Williamson (Cincinnati, OH: St. Anthony Messenger, 2006), p. 131.

6. Geffrey B. Kelly, "Karl Rahner's Reflections on the Love of Neighbor" *The Living Pulpit* 11, no. 3 (2002): 22–23.

7. Nanci Hellmich, "Santa Shares His Secret" *USA Today* (December 21, 2006).

Chapter 3. How Disciplined Are You?

1. William Barclay, a renowned scripture scholar, maintains that the devil was suggesting that Jesus bribe people by offering them material things.

2. Murray Bodo, OFM, *The Way of Francis* (Garden City, NY: Doubleday and Co. 1984), 21.

3. If you want more information see Cecile Andrews, *The Circle of Simplicity: The Return to the Good Life* (New York, NY: Harper Collins, 1997).

4. *Adbusters* encourages people to participate by not participating in shopping for a day. The campaign has spread to the United Kingdom, Europe, Asia, and the United States.

5. Lance Morrow, "The Search for Virtues" *Time* 143, 10 (1994): 78.

6. Michael Timmis, "Evangelizing in Business and Government," in *John Paul II and the New Evangelization,* eds. Ralph Martin and Peter Williamson (Cincinnati, OH: St. Anthony Messenger, 2006), p. 209.

7. Peter Gillquist, *Why We Haven't Changed the World* (New York: F.H. Revell Co. 1982), 56–57.

Chapter 4. Going Beyond Tolerance

1. Ralph Martin and Peter Williamson, eds., *John Paul II and the New Evangelization,* (Cincinnati, OH: St. Anthony Messenger, 2006), 127–28.

2. Keith A. Russell, "Why Does Someone Have to Win?" *The Living Pulpit* 12, no. 1 (2003): 17.

3. Keith A. Russell, "Is Tolerance Enough?" *The Living Pulpit* 12, no. 1 (2003): 1.

4. Brian J. Pierce, OP, "Welcoming the Strange New Word" *The Living Pulpit* 12, no. 1 (2003): 41.

Chapter 5. The Dark Side of Enmity

1. Bruce Chilton, "Jesus and the End of Enmity" *The Living Pulpit* 13, no. 1 (2004): 7.

2. Tim Flannery, *The Weather Makers* (New York: Grove Press, 2005), 56.

3. Rebecca Raddillo, "The Embodiment of Enmity" *The Living Pulpit* 13, no. 1 (2004): 37.

4. Keith Russell, "Refraining from Vengeance" *The Living Pulpit* 13, no. 1 (2004): 32.

5. Taken from Global News article by Peter Pophan, September 16, 2006.

6. Richard Rohr, OFM, *Hope Against Darkness* (Cincinnati, OH: St. Anthony Messenger, 2001), 163–64.

Chapter 6. Dare We *Care-front*?

1. David Augsburger, *Caring Enough to Confront* (Ventura, CA: Regal Books, 1983), 9–15.

2. Augsburger, *Caring Enough to Confront,* 53.

3. Robert Hoffman, *No One Is to Blame* (Palo Alto, CA: Science and Behavior Books Inc., 1979), 123–29.

4. Andrew Costello, *How to Deal with Difficult People* (Liguori, MO: Liguori Publications, 1970), 100–104.

5. Patrick Brennan, *Paschal Journey: Reflections on Psycho-Spiritual Growth* (Chicago, IL: Thomas More, 1992), 195.

Chapter 7. How Forgiving Are We?

1. Raniero Cantalamessa, OFM Cap, *Sober Intoxication of the Spirit,* trans. Marsha Daigle Williamson (Cincinnati, OH: St. Anthony Messenger, 2005), 109.

2. Eckhart Tolle, *The Power of Now* (Novato, CA: New World Library, 1999), 38.

3. Dawn Gibeau, "The Healing Power of Forgiving" *Praying* 90 (15 January 1999): 7.

Chapter 8. Is Attitude Everything?

1. Jeff Keller has a book by that title maintaining that if you change your attitude, you can change your life.

2. Ronald J. Sider, *The Scandal of the Evangelical Conscience* (Grand Rapids, MI: Baker Books, 2005), 122. He believes this question applies to contemporary American Evangelicals.

3. Alice Mathews, *Preaching That Speaks to Women* (Grand Rapids, MI: Baker Academic, 2003), 148–49.

4. Kenneth Boyack, CSP, "Go and Make Disciples: The United States Bishops' Plan for Catholic Evangelization," in *John Paul II and the New Evangelization,* eds. Ralph Martin and Peter Williamson (Cincinnati, OH: St. Anthony Messenger, 2006), p. 68.

Chapter 9. Conflicting Opinions on Wealth

1. Andre Resner, Jr. "Reading the Text for EcoNo.mic Justice: Mark 12:38–44 for Stewardship Season" *The Living Pulpit* 12, no. 2 (2003): 6–7.

2. Ched Meyers, "Why Sabbath Economics?" *The Living Pulpit* 12, no. 2 (2003): 14–15.

3. John W. Wimberly, Jr. "Sharing Versus Hoarding," *The Living Pulpit* 12, no. 2 (2003): 42–43.

4. *The Living Pulpit* 12, no. 2 (2003): 35.

5. Sider, *The Scandal of the Evangelical Conscience,* 20–22.

6. John Vaugn, "Show Me Your Money; I Will Show You Your Priorities," *The Living Pulpit* 12, no. 2 (2003): 10.

Chapter 10. Outsiders versus Insiders

1. "Quotations" *The Living Pulpit* 13, No. 3 (2004): 47.

2. Douglas S. Stivison, "Meeting Walter Burghardt" *The Living Pulpit* 13, (2004): 44.

3. "Quotations" *The Living Pulpit* 13, (2004): 47.

4. Mathews, *Preaching That Speaks to Women,* 144.

5. Sider, *The Scandal of the Evangelical Conscience,* 25–26.

6. C. Welton Gaddy, "Responding to Outsiders: A Spiritual Challenge, A Personal Pilgrimage" *The Living Pulpit* 13, No. 4 (2004): 22.

7. "Quotations" *The Living Pulpit* 13, No. 4 (2004): 47.

Chapter 11. Who Will Speak for Children?

1. Hedda Sharapan, "Think of Children First: What I Continue to Learn from Fred Rogers" *The Living Pulpit* 12, No. 4 (2003): 6.

2. Edwina Gateley, "The Gifts and Challenges of Parenting" *The Living Pulpit* 12, No. 4 (2003): 38.

3. More examples are found in Marian Wright Edelman, "A Parent, Community, and National Audit: Who Are Our Children Mirroring?" *The Living Pulpit* 12, no. 4 (2003): 8–9.

4. This was based on a news release, May 26, 2006.

5. Archbishop Timothy Dolan, "Church Cannot Let Up in Fight Against Sexual Abuse of Young" *Catholic Herald* 139, No. 17 (April 24, 2008): 2.

6. Donald W. Shriver, Jr., "Leave No Child Behind" *The Living Pulpit* 12, no. 4 (2003): 13.

7. Mary M. Doyle Roche, "A Little Child Will Lead Them" *The Living Pulpit* 12, no. 4 (2003): 14–15.

8. Donald W. Shriver, Jr., "Leave No Child Behind" *The Living Pulpit* 12, no. 4 (2003): 13.

Chapter 12. Becoming *"a Pray-er"*

1. Ronald Rolheiser, OMI, *Forgotten Among the Lilies* (New York, NY: Doubleday, 2005), 129.

2. May, *The Dark Night of the Soul,* 25.

3. Thomas Merton, *The Sign of Jonas* (New York: Harcourt, Brace and Co., 1953), 261.

4. Leonard Foley, OFM, and Pat McCloskey, OFM, eds., *Saint of the Day.* (Cincinnati, OH: St. Anthony Messenger, 2003), 41–42.

5. Jean Gill, *Pray as You Can* (Notre Dame, IN: Ave Maria Press, 1989), 44.

BIBLIOGRAPHY

Alison, James. *Faith Beyond Resentment*. New York: Crossroad, 2001.

Andrews, Cecile. *The Circle of Simplicity: The Return to the Good Life*. New York: Harper Collins, 1997.

Augsburger, David. *Caring Enough to Confront*. Ventura, CA: Regal Books, 1973.

Bennett, Oliver. *Cultural Pessimism: Narratives of Decline in the Post Modern World*. Edinburgh: Edinburgh University Press, 2001.

Bennett, William. *The Book of Virtues*. New York: Simon and Shuster, 1996.

Benthem, Vinal Van. *On the Way to Work*. Mystic, CT: Twenty-Third Publications, 2004.

Bloom, Anthony. *God and Man*. Westminster, MD: Newman Press, 1971.

Bodo, Murray, OFM. *The Way of Francis*. Garden City, NY: Doubleday and Co., 1984.

Brennan, Patrick. *Paschal Journey—Reflections on Psycho-Spiritual Growth*. Chicago, IL: Thomas More, 1992.

Burrows, Ruth. *Living in Mystery*. Danville, NJ: Dimension Books, 2000.

Cantalamessa, Raniero, OFM Cap. *Sober Intoxication of the Spirit*. Translated by Marsha Daigle Williamson. Cincinnati, OH: St. Anthony Messenger, 2005.

Casarjian, Robin. *Forgiveness: A Bold Choice for a Peaceful Heart*. New York: Bantam Books, 1992.

Catoir, John T. *Enjoy Your Precious Life*. Staten Island, NY: Alba House, 2003.

Chilton, Bruce. "Jesus and the End of Eternity." *The Living Pulpit* 13, no. 1 (2004): 7–9.

Coffin, William Sloan. *Credo*. Louisville, KY: John Knox Press, 2004.

Dillard, Annie. *For the Time Being*. New York: Random House, 1999.

Eck, Diana L. *A New Religious America*. New York: Harper Collins, 2001.

Ford, Michael, ed. *Eternal Seasons: A Liturgical Journey with Henri J.M. Nouwen*. Notre Dame, IN: Sorrin Books, 2004.

Gateley, Edwina. "The Gifts and Challenging of Parenting." *The Living Pulpit* 12, no. 4 (2003): 38–39.

Gilbert, William Schwenck. *Princess Ida*. 1884.

Gill, Jean. *Pray as You Can*. Notre Dame, IN: Ave Maria Press, 1989.

Gillquist, Peter. *Why We Haven't Changed the World*. New York: F.H. Revell Co., 1982.

Hillestad, E. Ann. "Offering the Good News." *America* 194 (20 February 2006): 19–21.

Hoffman, Robert. *No One is to Blame*. Palo Alto, CA: Science and Behavior Books, 1979.

Hughes, Bishop Alfred. *Spiritual Masters*. Huntington, IN: Our Sunday Visitor, 1998.

Keller, Jeff. *Attitude Is Everything*. Tampa, FL: International Network Training Institute, 1999.

Mahfood, Ferdinand. *Are You Serious?* Deerfield Beach, FL: Food for the Poor Inc., 1999.

Martin, James, SJ. *Good Company*. Franklin, WI: Sheed and Ward, 2000.

Martin, Ralph and Williamson, Peter, eds. *John Paul II and the New Evangelization*. Cincinnati, OH: Servant Books, 2006.

Merton, Thomas, OSCO. *Sign of Jonas*. New York, NY: Harcourt, Brace and Co. 1953.

Mathews, Alice P. *Preaching That Speaks to Women*. Grand Rapids, MI: Baker Books, 2003.

May, Gerald. *The Dark Night of the Soul*. San Francisco, CA: Harper, 1990.

Miller, Alice. *The Drama of the Gifted Child*. New York: Harper Collins, 2001.

Myers, Ched. "Why Sabbath Economics?" *The Living Pulpit* 12, no. 2 (2003): 14–15.

Nelson, Marcia Z. *The Gospel According to Oprah*. Louisville, KY: Westminster John Knox Press, 2005.

Pierce, Brian J. OP. "Welcome the Strange New Word." *The Living Pulpit* 12, no. 1 (2003): 40–41.

Pope Paul VI. *Ecclesiam Suam*. 1964.

Pope Benedict XVI. *Deus Caritas Est*. 2006.

"Quotations." *The Living Pulpit* 13, no. 4 (2004): 47–48.

Raddillo, Rebecca. "The Embodiment of Enmity." *The Living Pulpit* 13, no. 1 (2004): 36–37.

Resner, Andre Jr. "Reading the Text for Economic Justice: Mark 12:38 for Stewardship Season" *The Living Pulpit* 12, no. 2 (2003): 6–7.

Rivers, Robert, CSP. *From Maintenance to Mission*. New York/ Mahwah, NJ: Paulist Press, 2005.

Robbins, Anthony. *Unlimited Power*. New York: Fireside, 1986.

Roche, Mary Doyle. "A Little Child Will Lead Them." *The Living Pulpit* 12, no. 4 (2003): 14–15.

Rohr, Richard, OFM. *Hope Against Darkness*. Cincinnati, OH: St. Anthony Messenger, 2001.

Rolheiser, Ronald. *Forgotten Among the Lilies*. New York: Doubleday, 2005.

Rosen, Mark. *Thank You for Being Such a Pain*. New York: Three Rivers Press, 1998.

Rupp, Joyce. *Praying Our Goodbyes*. Notre Dame, IN: Ave Maria Press, 1968.

Russell, Keith. "Why Does Someone Have to Win?" *The Living Pulpit* 12, no. 2 (2003): 16–17.

————. "Refraining from Vengeance." *The Living Pulpit* 13 (2004): 32–33.

Sharapan, Hedda, "Think of Children First: What I Continue to Learn from Fred Rogers." *The Living Pulpit* 12 (2003): 6–7.

Shea, John. *Gospel Light*. Lanham, MD: National Book Network, 1998.

Shields, Ann, SGL. *Pray and Never Lose Hear: The Power of Intercession*. Cincinnati, OH: St. Anthony Messenger, 2001.

Sider, Ronald, J. *The Scandal of Evangelical Conscience*. Grand Rapids, MI: Baker Books, 2005.

Swindoll, Charles. *Swindoll's Ultimate Book of Illustrations and Quotes*. Nashville, TN: Thomas Nelson, Inc., 1998.

Tolle, Eckhart. *The Power of Now*. Novato, CA: New World Library, 1999.

Van Breemen, Peter, SJ. *The God Who Won't Let Go*. Notre Dame, IN: Ave Maria Press, 2001.

Velocci, Giovanni, CSSR. *Prayer in Newman*. Translated by Rev. Nicholas L Gregoris. Mount Pocono, PA: Newman Press, 2006.

Warren, Rick. *The Purpose Driven Life*. Grand Rapids, MI: Zondervan, 2002.

Welty, Eudora. *Eye of the Story*. New York: Random House, 1978.

Wimberly, John Jr. "Sharing vs Hoarding." *The Living Pulpit* 12, no. 2 (2003): 42–43.

Wuthnow, Robert. *American Mythos*. Princeton, NJ: Princeton University Press, 2006.